GUIDE FOR CELEBRATING®
MATRIMONY

PREPARING PARISH WORSHIP™

RICHARD B. HILGARTNER
DANIEL J. MERZ

LTP

LITURGY
TRAINING
PUBLICATIONS

Nihil Obstat
Very Reverend Ronald A. Hicks
Vicar for Canonical Services
Archdiocese of Chicago
April 25, 2016

Imprimatur
Most Reverend Francis J. Kane, DD
Vicar General
Archdiocese of Chicago
April 25, 2016

The *Nihil Obstat* and *Imprimatur* are declarations that the material is free from doctrinal or moral error, and thus is granted permission to publish in accordance with c. 827. No legal responsibility is assumed by the grant of this permission. No implication is contained herein that those who have granted the *Nihil Obstat* and *Imprimatur* agree with the content, opinions, or statements expressed.

The "Glossary" definitions were written by Corinna Laughlin, Dennis C. Smolarski, SJ, and Joseph DeGrocco. The "Resources" section was written by Sandra Dooley.

This book was edited by Danielle A. Noe, MDIV. Christopher Magnus was the production editor, Anna Manhart was the designer, and Kari Nicholls was the production artist.

Photos on page 90 © Russ Clepper; pages 19 and 24 by Michelle Hartman; photo on page 72 © Stacey Jackson; pages 73, 78, 82, and 94 by Andrew Kennedy Lewis © Liturgy Training Publications; pages 32, 44, 45, and 70 © Sheena Magnesen; pages 31, 59, 76, and 95 © Joanna Pach/Darling Moments Photography; pages 14, 23, 30, 49, and 65 © Rush Photography and Video; pages 26, 41, 48, 53, 74, 75, 99, and 101 © John Zich; page 69 © Liturgy Training Publications.

Art on page vi © Martin Erspamer, OSB. The photo on page 15 courtesy of William and Katherine Sperry.

20   19   18   17   16   1   2   3   4   5

Printed in the United States of America.

Library of Congress Control Number: 2016941904

ISBN 978-1-61671-237-2

EGCM

CONTENTS

PREFACE

D on't you mean, 'We're out of water'?" asked Nereus, drying his hands. "I just emptied this jar washing up. What do you mean we're out of wine?"

"Just what I said," responded Rufus.

"But I thought we had enough."

"For this many people?"

Nereus looked around the courtyard. "Who are all these people?"

"You don't know? Aren't you the groom? Didn't you invite them?"

Nereus recognized Mary, as well as her son, Jesus. He was expecting them. But Jesus was surrounded by a group of young men. Nereus said softly to Rufus, "He brought his disciples?"

Jesus looked up, as if he heard every word. Then Nereus remembered, "Oh, that's right. I told him they could come."

He watched a scene unfolding over the shoulder of Jesus' mother. Urbanus, another server like Rufus, was exchanging words with Herodion, the guest who had traveled all the way from Dan to Cana. Mary anxiously moved closer toward her son. But James and John were commanding his attention.

Rufus explained, "Everyone's blaming the servers. But we're doing our job. We've been pouring wine and filling glasses for the last hour. There are a lot of glasses. After all, it's a wedding."

Nereus could not afford any trouble on his wedding day. It wasn't the servers' fault. He summoned Tertius, the headwaiter. "Can you get more wine?"

"Shops are closed," he said. "Don't you have any more here?"

"Excuse me," said Rufus. "Now even the women are starting to complain." Nereus looked up to see Jesus' mother summoning the server. Rufus took a deep breath and walked toward her. He signaled Urbanus to join him.

"Excuse me," Urbanus said to Herodion. "The other server needs me." He skipped away, happy to be out of the spat.

As Rufus and Urbanus approached, Mary reached into the group of disciples and grabbed her son's elbow. "They have no wine."[1]

James and John looked at Mary, then at Jesus, and then at the diminishing contents of their glasses.

"You always were a great drinker," James smirked at John. "I'm not the greatest," said John. "You're the greatest."

Jesus rolled his eyes and shook his head. Turning from his disciples, he folded his arms and stared at his mother. "Woman, how does your concern affect me? My hour has not yet come."[2]

It was getting late, but Urbanus had no idea what hour Jesus meant. Mary turned her gaze away from Jesus and toward the servants. "Do whatever he tells you."[3] Jesus tightened his lips and set his jaw. Exasperated, he said to the servants. "Fill the jars with water."[4]

Urbanus and Rufus looked back toward Nereus and Tertius, still standing away from the growing hubbub near the place where he had washed his hands. Six stone water jars stood there, empty after all the guests had washed.

Rufus bowed to Jesus and walked away. Urbanus ran after him. "Wait a minute. Since when do we take orders from a guest? We work for Nereus." Then, looking at his friend's transfixed face, Urbanus asked, "What's the matter with you?"

"You take that end, I'll get the other," intoned Rufus. It took both of them to carry the jars empty. Filled with water, each would weigh more than 200 pounds. "Can anybody help us?" Urbanus cried.

"I can," said James. "I'm the greatest." "No, you're not," said John. "I am. Wait, I'll help."

---

1 John 2:3.
2 John 2:4.
3 John 2:5.
4 John 2:7.

The four of them, staggering under the jars, carried them one by one back into the courtyard. Jesus said to them, "Draw some out now and take it to the headwaiter."[5]

Rufus took a ladle, dipped it into the water, and pulled it out. "It's red," he gasped. He ran to Tertius.

"What's this?" he asked. "Here," said Rufus. "Taste this." Tertius looked at the ladle and drew back his head. "Just taste it." Tertius sipped the water that had become wine. "Nereus, you dog!" he said, a smile broadening his face. He slapped the bridegroom on the shoulder. "Good joke, Nereus! You were holding out on me." He pointed to the six water jars. "You had plenty of wine all along. The laugh is on me." Nereus cocked his head and quizzically looked at Rufus, but he said nothing. "There's just one thing I can't figure out," said the headwaiter. "Everyone serves good wine first, and then when people have drunk freely, an inferior one; but you have kept the good wine until now."[6]

Rufus looked up and saw Jesus leaving the courtyard together with his mother and his disciples. Rufus walked over and joined the group.

"Rufus," said Nereus, "where are you going? Stay, man. Have some wine." But Rufus kept walking after Jesus. "Rufus, this is a wedding. It's a party. What could be more important than my wedding?"

—Paul Turner

PAUL TURNER is pastor of St. Anthony Parish in Kansas City, Missouri. A priest of the Diocese of Kansas City-St. Joseph, he holds a doctorate in sacred theology from Sant'Anselmo in Rome. He has published many pastoral resources.

---

5 John 2:8.
6 John 2:10.

WELCOME

The celebration of the Sacrament of Matrimony is one of the most significant moments in the lives of spouses-to-be as they enter into their God-given vocation and give their lives to one another. They become a sign of God's love and a manifestation of his grace for each other and for the world. Pastoral ministers who work with couples share in their joy and have a unique perspective to witness the movement of God's grace in them.

For pastoral ministers who accompany, assist, and prepare couples for Marriage, however, the process of Marriage preparation can, in the midst of grace, be filled with difficulties, challenges, and frustrations. Effective Marriage preparation requires a commitment of time and effort from a variety of parish ministers: clergy who preside at the Marriage celebration and meet with couples for months in advance; pastoral musicians who dedicate time for preparing and rehearsing to meet special requests of couples; Marriage preparation teams, especially "sponsor couples" who open their homes and meet extensively with engaged couples for catechetical formation; and even parish office managers, administrative assistants, sacristans, and parish wedding coordinators who are key team members assisting couples with the details of scheduling and preparing their Marriage liturgy.

About This Book

This book is addressed to all those who work with couples preparing for Marriage: clergy, pastoral musicians, Marriage preparation teams, sacristans, and others who have any contact with the couple. It aims to encourage the use of sound liturgical practices for the celebration of *The Order of Celebrating Matrimony*, and to provide a framework for effective pastoral outreach during the Marriage preparation process—from the first moment of inquiry by engaged couples to what might take place "post-Cana" as a means of mystagogical catechesis in the spirit of the New Evangelization.

After setting the historical context and the theology of Christian Marriage practices and the development of *The Order for Celebrating Matrimony* as we know it today, this book will provide detailed explanations of the various elements of the rituals as found in the newly-promulgated second edition of *The Order of Celebrating Matrimony.*

The *Constitution on the Sacred Liturgy*[1] of the Second Vatican Council suggested that inculturation of the liturgy could be an effective means of fostering the full, conscious, and active participation of the faithful. *The Order of Celebrating Matrimony*, in a particular way, makes extensive use of rituals and symbols that have particular cultural roots, and the ritual text gives the Conference of Bishops the authority to adapt and to make additions to the ritual text. While a variety of cultural adaptations have been included in *The Order of Celebrating Matrimony* for use in the dioceses of the United States, one of the pastoral challenges in the celebration of the Sacrament of Matrimony is the way in which the practices and expectations of secular culture influence—or are at times at odds with—the Church's ritual. This book will attempt to address the delicate process of introducing couples to liturgical and sacramental principles.

Finally, this book will suggest ways in which parishes can renew or re-invigorate their approach to Marriage preparation as a team approach that includes the ministry not only of clergy, pastoral musicians, and Marriage preparation teams but all those who will assist and interact with engaged couples, including the members of the liturgical assembly.

About the Authors

Msgr. Richard B. Hilgartner is a priest of the Archdiocese of Baltimore. He is a graduate of Mount St. Mary's University, Emmitsburg, Maryland, and St. Mary's Seminary, Baltimore. He completed an stl in Liturgical and Sacramental Theology at the Pontifical Athenaeum of Sant'Anselmo in Rome, where he has also begun pursuing a doctorate in Sacramental and Liturgical Theology. From 2007 to 2014 he served at the U.S. Conference of Catholic Bishops' Secretariat of Divine Worship, first as associate director, and then as executive director. There, he helped prepare for and oversaw the

---

1 *Constitution on the Sacred Liturgy* (CSL), 37: "Even in the liturgy the Church has no wish to impose a rigid uniformity in matters that do not affect the faith or the good of the whole community; rather, the Church respects and fosters the genius and talents of the various races and peoples. The Church considers with sympathy and, if possible, preserves intact the elements in these peoples' way of life that are not indissolubly bound up with superstition and error. Sometimes in fact the Church admits such elements into the liturgy itself, provided they are in keeping with the true and authentic spirit of the liturgy."

implementation of the third edition of *The Roman Missal* in 2011. Msgr. Hilgartner served in several parishes in Baltimore, as chaplain and director of campus ministry at Mount St. Mary's University, and he also taught homiletics at St. Mary's Seminary. He now serves as pastor at St. Joseph's Parish in Cockeysville, Maryland, and concurrently serves as president of the National Association of Pastoral Musicians (NPM).

REV. DANIEL J. MERZ was ordained a priest of the Jefferson City Diocese in Missouri in 1998. He completed an SLD (Doctorate in Sacred Liturgy) at the Pontifical Institute of Liturgy in Rome in 2011. From 2001 to 2011, he taught at Conception Seminary College. He served in the Secretariat of Divine Worship for the USCCB from 2011 to 2014, and is currently pastor of two parishes in his diocese. During his time at the USCCB, in collaboration with Msgr. Hilgartner, he helped with the implementation of *The Roman Missal*. He has published several articles on the liturgy, and coauthored with Abbot Marcel Rooney: *Essential Presidential Prayers and Texts: A Roman Missal Study Edition and Workbook*, published by Liturgy Training Publications.

The Theological and Historical Developments of the Catholic Marriage Ritual

"I will betroth you to me forever."

—Hosea 2:21

t is clear that the institution of marriage predates Christianity as well as Judaism. One of the Nuptial Blessings still mentions Marriage as, "the one blessing / not forfeited by original sin / nor washed away by the flood."[1] It belongs to the order of creation, the order of nature and natural law, and original sin never prevailed against it. This is proved by the fact that the manner of effecting marriages has more to do with social customs and practices than with divine revelation. Divine revelation impacts the Christian theology of Marriage, but the way of effecting this institution between a man and a woman is mostly found in social customs. The 1983 *Code of Canon Law* acknowledges the natural bond and institution of marriage, while also stating that when both spouses are baptized, Marriage is elevated to a sacrament:

> The matrimonial covenant, by which a man and a woman establish a lifelong partnership between themselves, derives its force and strength from creation, but for the Christian faithful it is also raised up to a higher dignity, since it is numbered among the Sacraments of the new covenant.
>
> —*The Order of Celebrating Matrimony*, 1.

"The matrimonial covenant, by which a man and a woman establish between themselves a partnership of the whole of life and which is ordered by its nature to the good of the spouses and the procreation and education of offspring, has been raised by Christ the Lord to the dignity of a sacrament between the baptized."[2]

---

1 *The Order of Celebrating Matrimony* (OCM), 74.
2 *Code of Canon Law* (CIC), 1055 §1.

Thus, the sacramentality of Marriage is something which strengthens and enriches the natural marital bond.

Because Marriage is first a natural bond that comes to us from the Creator, it is understandable that the rituals surrounding Marriage over the centuries have been primarily a domestic affair with substantial variations depending on the time and place. To understand the current Roman Rite for celebrating Marriage, an examination of the customs and practices of the early Romans is important.

Roman Customs

The anonymous *Letter to Diognetus* (late first, early second century) makes a passing comment that "Christians marry like everyone else."[3] The author knows of nothing unusual about Christian Marriage as distinct from pagan marriage—though the explicitly pagan elements were assuredly removed (for example, consulting the auspices, sacrificing to the gods, and the licentious aspects of feasting and processions).

From ancient times up until the fourth century (for pagans, Jews, and Christians), there were two clearly distinct moments in time: a betrothal period established by a *stipulatio* (agreement, contract), and then the marriage ceremony itself. The betrothal period, which is found in Scripture,[4] was established by a meeting between the suitor and the girl's father in order to agree on the formalities of the marriage ceremonies and especially on the dowry. Oftentimes a banquet would follow the agreement, and later the customs of the giving of a ring and the joining of right hands were included.[5]

Stipulatio

The *stipulatio* was a meeting between the two family heads.[6] The negotiations were not simply about the union of two individuals, but the union of two families, which could have a great social and political impact, depending on the

---

3 *Ad Diognetum* 5, 6, ed. H. I. Marrou, Sources Chrétiennes, 2nd ref., vol. 33 (Paris: Cerf, 1965), pp. 62–63.

4 See, for example, Genesis 29:18, Deuteronomy 20:7, Matthew 1:18, and Luke 1:27.

5 See *Handbook for Liturgical Studies*, vol. 4, *Sacraments and Sacramentals*, ed. Anscar J. Chupungco (Liturgical Press: Collegeville, MN, 2000), 276ff. See also *The Church at Prayer: An Introduction to the Liturgy*, vol. 3, *The Sacraments*, ed. A.G. Martimort (The Liturgical Press: Collegeville, MN, 1988), p. 186ff.

6 See Tobit 7:12–14.

wealth and prominence of the families. With the Roman Empire, this agreement became a true contract, legally recognized and with binding legal force.

Dowry

The dowry is an ancient custom and was also present in the first rituals of the Latin Church. It was an advance payment by the girl's father on her inheritance and remained her property throughout the marriage, although the husband could profit from its interest. It was seen as a public commitment to the marriage.

Dexterarum iunctio

Dexterarum iunctio means the "joining of the right hands" and was added to the ritual around the first century BC. The gesture of the joining of the right hands was a public symbol of the joining of the two individuals, but more importantly, the joining of two families. The one officiating the joining would have varied over the ages: the girl's father, an older married woman, or later, the Christian priest. There is a sarcophagus dating to AD 382 that depicts a young couple in the act of joining their right hands, and the figure behind them doing the joining is none other than Christ himself. This also came to be called the *traditio puellae*, the handing over of the girl.

Iron Ring

The ring was normally an iron ring, simple and devoid of any precious stones. It was first mentioned by Pliny in the first century AD and was a symbol of public commitment on behalf of the groom to the bride. Iron stood for the strength of commitment by the groom. The simplicity of a ring without precious stones would make it stand out as different from any other jewelry the girl might wear, and quickly and easily mark her out as betrothed.

On the day of the marriage, most of the ritual was centered on the bride. For pagan Rome, this could include the following rituals:

1. A rite of passage in which she surrendered her playthings and child-age clothing (dedicating them to the household gods of her family).

2. A new identity, symbolized by the following:

   - The *tutulus*: a special hairstyle that evoked Rome's ancient Etruscan past and honored the gods Jupiter and Juno (the wife of the *flamen dialis*, high priest of Jupiter, always wore her hair in the *tutulus* style).

- The *flammeum*: a veil, deep yellow in color, like the flame of a candle. This demonstrated modesty, a shift to matronly virtues, and also imitated the attire of the wife of the *flamen dialis*. This went on to become one of the main symbols of the wedding ceremony. The Latin verb "to marry," *nubo, nubere*, is related to the noun *nubes* (a cloud) and literally means "I veil myself." The wedding ceremony is now focused on the bride and her veiling.

- An *amaracus* wreath: a sweet-scented floral wreath that was worn on the bride's head as a sign of freshness, life, and beauty. For the pagans, it also imitated the gods and goddesses, which is why Christians initially shunned the use of crowns in weddings.

- *Tunica recta* and *cingulum*: the bride dressed in a simple white tunic (matronly and pure) that was cinctured with a girdle. For the pagans, the girdle was tied with a special, complicated knot called a herculean knot, evoking the virility of Hercules, who was said to have fathered seventy children. This knot was at the waist of her dress and was to be undone by her husband alone after she entered the bridal chamber in his house (the phrase "tying the knot" seems to be descended from this practice).

3. A procession from the house of the bride's family to the groom's house conveyed that she was no longer under the authority of the *pater familias* (household father). The initial ceremonies, including a banquet,[7] would all take place at the house of the bride's family. The procession to the groom's house,[8] typically late at night, was often accompanied by raucous and bawdy singing, shouting, and joke-telling. In entering the groom's house, she was placing herself under his authority as the *pater familias* of a new household. There, she would be led into the bridal chamber, the groom would untie the herculean knot, and the rest would withdraw leaving the bride and groom alone.[9]

4. Upon arrival at the groom's house (again, among the pagans), the groom would present the bride with fire and water, symbols of her duties to tend to new household gods and a new hearth.

5. In addition to honoring Jupiter and Juno indirectly through the bride's attire, the couple would often pay for a priest to offer a sacrifice to Jupiter.

---

7 See John 2:1–11.
8 See Judges 14:11; 1 Maccabees 9:39; and Matthew 25:1–13.
9 See Tobit 7:16; 8:1, 4.

Jewish Customs

Another part of the ancient wedding ceremony that continues into the contemporary period in some places is the wedding canopy. Jewish sources refer to this as the *huppa veil*. This canopy would be placed over both spouses, and was intended to evoke the image of a household roof. In marriage, the couple is building a new household. In Jewish commentary, this canopy evokes the weight of glory of the divine *shekinah*.[10] In Christian commentary, the canopy evokes the overshadowing of the Holy Spirit, who binds the two as one and makes them fruitful. Psalm 19:6 speaks of the sun rising for the day like a bridegroom emerging from his *huppa*, his bridal chamber, after consummating the night with his bride. There is an interesting reference to the canopy (or tent) in Joel 2:16, although here it is in the context of the great and terrible "Day of the Lord," which claims priority over all, "Let the bridegroom emerge from his chamber [*chedro*], and the bride from her *huppa*." In other words, if the "Day of the Lord" comes before the groom can enter the *huppa* to consummate with his bride, then priority must be given to the "Day of the Lord" over consummating the marriage. A New Testament reference is found in Revelation 21:2, which describes what could be called the eschatological bridal chamber: "I also saw the holy city, a new Jerusalem, coming down out of heaven from God, prepared as a bride adorned for her husband." This is a description after the consummation, because the groom—the Lamb—is already with the bride in the city, and the whole city is portrayed as the bridal chamber.

Marriage in the Old Testament

There are four dimensions of Marriage in Old Testament biblical revelation:[11]

1. Marriage is both unitive[12] and procreative.[13]

> The LORD God said: It is not good for the man to be alone. I will make a helper suited to him.
>
> —Genesis 2:18

---

10 Although not found in the Old Testament, this word describes the appearance of divine glory in time, its shining forth, or settling upon God's people or creation.

11 See *Handbook for Liturgical Studies*, vol. 4, *Sacraments and Sacramentals*, ed. Anscar J. Chupungco (Liturgical Press: Collegeville, MN, 2000), p. 276ff. See also *The Church at Prayer: An Introduction to the Liturgy*, vol. 3, *The Sacraments*, ed. A.G. Martimort (The Liturgical Press: Collegeville, MN, 1988), pp. 282-283.

12 See Genesis 2:18.

13 See Genesis 1:28.

2. Marriage is covenantal: Especially with the prophets, the archetype for marriage becomes the covenant between God and Israel, and this gives it a juridic aspect. But the covenant also brings the model of love into marriage. Deuteronomy 7:7–8 speaks of marriage as a matter of love and fidelity and Hosea 2:20–22 speaks of God's covenant with Israel as a marriage.

3. Marriage comes to be seen as indissoluble: Malachi 2:14–16 goes beyond the Mosaic Law which allowed for divorce, calling for the two to become one both in the flesh and in the spirit. Here, the pleasures of love are only to be had in the context of fidelity. With the Book of Tobit,[14] lawful marriage is even seen as a matter of salvation, of life and death. The love between Tobiah and Sarah is salvific because it is chaste, sanctified by prayer, and able to be continent.

4. Marriage is a sign of eschatological unity: In the Song of Songs, the lover and the beloved describe their relationship in such idyllic terms as to evoke the perfection of Adam and Eve in Paradise. As the one blessing not forfeited by original sin or washed away in the flood, Marriage retains the power to evoke the original innocence of Eden: "[M]y dove, my perfect one, / her mother's special one, / favorite of the one who bore her. / Daughters see her and call her happy, / queens and concubines, and they praise her."[15]

Marriage in the New Testament

There are two major differences regarding Marriage in light of Jesus Christ. First, the ideal of human existence and relationships have been realized in Christ, and second, the protagonists in sacramental Marriage have been changed—transformed—by entering into the sacrament. First, Marriage is no longer merely the archetype for the covenant; it is the sacrament of the covenant. In the wedding feast at Cana in John 2, the jars filled with water are reminders of the Jewish rites of purification that belonged to the old covenant. With Jesus, however, they contain wine—the sign of the new covenant in the blood of Jesus Christ. During this event, Christ explicitly evokes his Passion by referring to his "hour." Christian Marriage is distinct because it sacramentalizes the "hour" of Christ on the Cross, our redemption, the Paschal Mystery of Christ.

---

14 See Tobit 8:4ff.

15 Song of Songs 6:9.

In Ephesians 5:21–32, St. Paul discusses Christian Marriage, and in verse 32 refers to Christian Marriage as a *mysterion mega*, a "great mystery," which he says refers ultimately to Christ and the Church. The union of husband and wife is a Christian reality precisely because it is a sacrament of Christ's sacrificial love for his bride, the Church, and the respectful obedience of the Church back to Christ.

The second difference in Christian Marriage is equally profound. Because of Baptism into Christ, the protagonists in Marriage have become Temples for the indwelling of the Holy Spirit. In the Old Testament, people are often filled with the Spirit of God to accomplish a specific task, but the language of indwelling is never used. That is a New Testament concept and reality. It is the reality of grace, which requires constant acceptance and surrender, but which also makes possible what was not possible before. The Second Vatican Council's document *Gaudium et spes* speaks powerfully to this new reality in Christ:

> The sacrament of marriage is not a social convention, an empty ritual or merely the outward sign of a commitment. The sacrament is a gift given for the sanctification and salvation of the spouses, since "their mutual belonging is a real representation, through the sacramental sign, of the same relationship between Christ and the Church. The married couple are therefore a permanent reminder for the Church of what took place on the cross."
>
> —*Amoris laetitia*, 72; quoting *Familiaris consortio*, 13

"Authentic married love is caught up into divine love and is governed and enriched by the redemptive power of Christ and the salvific action of the church, with the result that the spouses are effectively led to God and are helped and strengthened in their lofty role as fathers and mothers. Spouses, therefore, are fortified and, as it were, consecrated for the duties and dignity of their state by a special sacrament; fulfilling their conjugal and family role by virtue of this sacrament, spouses are penetrated with the spirit of Christ and their whole life is suffused by faith, hope and charity; thus they increasingly further their own perfection and their mutual sanctification, and together they render glory to God."[16]

> Infused by the Holy Spirit, this powerful love is a reflection of the unbroken covenant between Christ and humanity that culminated in his self-sacrifice on the cross.
>
> — *Amoris laetitia*, 120

---

16 *Gaudium et spes* (GS), 48.

Matthew 19:6 makes known that the hardness of heart that Moses had to deal with has been overcome in Christ and so divorce is no longer an option for the Christian. In Matthew 19:10, his disciples realize that Marriage is not easy: if divorce and remarriage mean adultery, then it is better not to marry! And Jesus' reply emphasizes that Christian Marriage is impossible without God, without the Holy Spirit.

Eastern Rites

Before examining the development of Marriage Rites in the West, a quick look at the central event in the wedding ceremony in the Eastern rites is helpful, especially because the Roman Rite foresees the crowning of the couple as something that could be requested and used also in the West.[17] In the Eastern Rites, the priest crowns the couple as a sign of their union. St. John Chrysostom wrote that the crowns symbolize the victory of Christ over sin, death, and evil. The spouses, as baptized Christians, lawfully joined in a sacramental Marriage, share in this victory. The crowns also symbolize the crown of martyrdom or witnessing to Christ, for the couple incarnates the love between Christ and the Church. Furthermore, the crowns represent the royal authority of the children of God (who are priest, prophet, and king by virtue of Baptism). The priest crowns the bridegroom and bride with the formula: "The servant of God, **N.**, is crowned unto the handmaiden of God, **N.**: in the name of the Father, and of the Son, and of the Holy Spirit."[18] A coronation hymn (Psalm 8:6, 7) is then sung: "O Lord our God, crown them with glory and honor."[19] After all of the prayers and ceremonies have been accomplished, the crowns are removed, and God is asked to preserve their crowns and Marriage forever in his Kingdom. Thus, the ceremony of crowning is shown to be the joining of two as one flesh for the purpose of helping each other to attain the crown of eternal life in heaven.

Western Rites

There are three main divisions that mark the development of Christian Marriage in the West:

---

17 See OCM, 41, 5: "After the giving of rings, in keeping with local customs, the crowning of the bride or the veiling of the spouses may take place."

18 Translation from John Meyendorff, *Marriage: An Orthodox Perspective*, 3rd rev. ed. (St. Vladimir's Seminary Press: Crestwood, New York, 1984), p. 124.

19 Meyendorff, p. 124.

1. The Marriage ceremony occurred in the family home until the eleventh century (and then the couple could go to the Church for a special Mass and the bride would receive a blessing).

2. The Marriage ceremony occurred at the doors of the church (*in facie ecclesiae*) beginning in the eleventh century. This is the first clear evidence of the rite of the sacrament itself, which was then followed by Mass and the Nuptial Blessing. The Council of Trent moved the ceremony into the church, but kept it prior to the Mass.

3. The Second Vatican Council placed the rite within Mass after the Liturgy of the Word, with the Nuptial Blessing after the Our Father, just before the reception of Communion.

Fourth to Tenth Centuries

For the first three centuries after Christ, there is no evidence that Christians had recourse to the use of a priest in weddings; nor do we have records of specifically Christian prayers. A properly structured ritual for Christian weddings does not appear before the eleventh century.

In his treatise *Ad uxorem*,[20] written in the third century, Tertullian writes of Christian Marriage as the icon of the union of Christ and the Church. He makes several statements, which are more theological than ritual in nature, but which may allude to some ritual ceremonies:

> "Joined by the Church, strengthened by a sacrificial offering, sealed by a blessing, announced by Angels, and ratified by the Father. . . . How wonderful the bond of the two believers: one in hope, one in vow, one in discipline, one in the same service! They are both children of one Father and servants of the same Master, with no separation of spirit and flesh. Indeed, they are two in one flesh; where there is one flesh, there is also one spirit."[21]

The earliest description of Christian Marriage in the West comes from an ode by St. Paulinus of Nola[22] written for the wedding of a Church lector, Julian, son of the bishop of Benevento, to Titia, daughter of the bishop of Capua. It proclaims a very sober vision of both the Marriage rite practiced among Roman Christians and the ideal they aspired to. The wedding takes place in the Church, but probably only because Julian was a lector. Regulations

---

20 See Tertullian, *Ad uxorem*, in *Corpus Christianorum*, Series Latina, 1:371–394.

21 Tertullian, *Ad uxorem* II, 8, 6–7 and 9, in *Corpus Christianorum*, Series Latina, 1:393–394; as quoted in OCM, 11.

22 See St. Paulinus, *Carmen* 25, in *Corpus Scriptorum Ecclesiasticum Latinorum*, 30:244–245.

requiring a blessing by the Church originated in the fifth century with clerical Marriages and were later extended to all Christians in the West. Julian and Titia's wedding includes classical Roman elements (the *dexterarum iunctio* and the nuptial veil) and Christian elements (hymn singing, prayers of blessing and consecration). There is no mention of an exchange of rings or vows (these would probably have taken place earlier in the home), or of the celebration of the Eucharist. There is a decided emphasis on the holiness of the baptized, a conscious distancing from the "secular display" of pagan marriages, an accent on simplicity, modesty, and above all, submission to the law of Christ. Stress is given to the shared life of holiness and that the couple is marrying "in Christ." Other themes include:

- the marriage of Adam and Eve as a prototype;
- allusion to the marriage of the Patriarchs;
- reference to the transcendence of gender differences in Baptism and to the unity of Christ and his Church, symbolized in Marriage;
- that the couple are children of the Church, brother and sister in Christ;
- and that the couple is preparing for the "yet greater nuptials" in the Kingdom of God.

Pope Siricius in the late fourth century emphasizes the *velatio* (that is, the canopy veil, or *huppa*, which was placed over the spouses during the nuptial blessing) as a quasisacramental rite.[23] This was distinct from the veil worn by the bride. He also emphasizes the importance of the priest's presence for this blessing. Previously, blessings and prayers were said by the bride's father. The veil came to carry the meaning of a type of epicletic moment, or an overshadowing of the Holy Spirit, as well as the protection of the Church's blessing over the couple.

The earliest texts related to Marriage are all linked to Mass formularies and are mostly Roman. The first comes from the collection called the *Veronense Sacramentary* (compiled between the fifth and seventh centuries) under the title *Velatio nuptialis* (nuptial veiling). The *Old Gelasian Sacramentary* (seventh century) uses the title *Actio nuptialis* (nuptial action), and the *Gregorian Hadrianum Sacramentary* (eighth century) has *Orationes ad sponsas velandas* (orations for veiling the spouses). The prayers found in these collections are all Mass formularies, including a Nuptial Blessing, but they

---

23 See Pope Siricius, *Epistle* 7, in *Patrologia Latina*, 13:117.

all emphasize the veil (nuptial) blessing as the unique element. The formula of blessing is very biblical, with references to women from the Old Testament. A translation of the text from the *Veronense Sacramentary* follows:

"Father, creator of the world, you gave life to every living creature and commissioned man to multiply. With your own hands, you gave Adam a companion: bones grown from his bones, to signify identity of form yet wondrous diversity. Thus your command to share the marriage bed, to increase and multiply in marriage, has linked the whole world together and established ties among the whole human race. This you saw, O Lord, to be pleasing, even necessary: that she who would be much weaker than man— she being made in his image, but he being made in yours—once joined to the stronger sex, they who were previously two become one; while from that oneness of love both sexes derive. Thus it was that generation was to follow generation, those who came first being succeeded by those who come after; so that humankind, though destined for death, and despite life's brevity, goes on without end. To this end, then, Father, bless the youth of your handmaid who is to marry. Joined in a good and blessed union, may she observe the mandates of the eternal law. May she remember that she is called not so much to the lawful pleasures of marriage as to the safeguarding of her promise of fidelity. May she marry in Christ as one faithful and chaste. May she prove loving to her husband, like Rachel; wise, like Rebecca; long-lived and faithful, like Sarah. May the author of lies never subvert her behavior; may she adhere steadfastly to the bond of fidelity and to the commandments. May discipline lend strength to her frailty as she devoutly serves the living God. Loyal to one bed, may she flee all unlawful relations. May she be serious and modest, her honor above reproach, instructed in the wisdom of heaven. May she be fruitful with children, a person of integrity and innocence. And may she come at last to enjoy the repose of the blessed and to the heavenly kingdom."[24]

God has given Adam a companion like himself, yet at the same time different. Both form the foundation of a great covenant of the human race with God. The prayer prays for the sanctification of the bride and concludes on an eschatological note, asking that the bride "enjoy the repose" of the blessed and arrive at the heavenly Kingdom. The Nuptial Blessings in the *Old Gelasian Sacramentary* and in the *Gregorian Sacramentary* are based on this prayer from the *Veronense Sacramentary*, though the *Gregorian Sacramentary*

---

24 *Veronense* XXXI, 1105–1110; translated in Mark Searle and Kenneth W. Stevenson, *Documents of the Marriage Liturgy* (The Liturgical Press: Collegeville, MN, 1992), pp. 42–44.

changes it the most. In the *Old Gelasian Saramentary*, the direct object of the prayer of blessing is the bride and primarily her fertility. It also insists on the mutual union of the spouses: *affectu compari* (with equal affection), *mente consimili* (of similar mind), *sanctitate mutua* (with mutual holiness). This prayer was given before the kiss of peace and followed by Communion.

One of the other Mass prayers that is important to highlight for its theological value is the Preface first found in the *Old Gelasian Sacramentary*. It refers to Marriage as a covenant and an indissoluble bond effected by God. It emphasizes a theological end for the procreative dimension of Marriage: the act of procreation is a collaboration in spreading the Kingdom by increasing the number of adoptive children for the Kingdom of Heaven. It concludes: "May that which birth has brought forth to enrich the world lead, by rebirth, to the growth of the Church."[25]

The *Gregorian Sacramentary*, compiled around the eighth century but with much earlier material, expands the prayer of blessing from the *Veronense Sacramentary*. The expansions have found their way into the contemporary rite:

> "O God, you have consecrated the bond of marriage with such an excellent mystery as to prefigure in the covenant of marriage the sacrament of Christ and his Church. O God, through you a woman is joined to her husband and society is chiefly ordered by that blessing which was neither lost by original sin nor washed away in the flood."[26]

It makes mention of Marriage as a mystery (*mysterio*) that prefigures (*praesignares*) the sacrament of Christ and the Church. This is the theology of St. Paul from his letter to the Ephesians. The second part of the prayer makes mention of the belief that Marriage was part of God's original plan before Adam's fall. In other words, for as long as God has been faithful to the human race, he calls man and woman to be faithful to each other.

Eleventh Century to the Second Vatican Council

In 1012, at the Synod of the Province of Rouen in France, canon 14 stated that in order to ensure the reality of Marriage as a public act, all Marriages

---

25 L.C. Mohlberg, *Liber Sacramentorum Romanae Ecclesiae Ordinis Anni Circuli (Gelasianum Vetus)*, RED Series Maior, Fontes IV (Rome, 1981), cf. 1446 (author's translation).

26 J. Deshusses, *Le Sacramentaire Grégorien*, vol. 3, Spicilegium Friburgense 28 (Fribourg, 1979), cf. 838a. Translation from Mark Searle and Kenneth W. Stevenson, *Documents of the Marriage Liturgy* (Collegeville, MN: The Liturgical Press, 1992), p. 48.

must be performed *in facie ecclesiae*, that is, before the doors of the church. The following is a description of this rite from an early twelfth-century Missal:

"The priest, vested in alb and stole and carrying holy water, is to take his place in front of the church door. After sprinkling the couple he is to question them in a prudent manner to find out whether they are resolved to marry in accordance with the law; he will make sure that they are not related, and he will instruct them on how they are to live together in the Lord.

"Next, following custom, he tells the parents to give their daughter to the groom, and tells the groom to give her dowry, the record of which he then reads out in the presence of all those attending. The priest has her marry him with a ring that is blessed in the name of the holy Trinity and that he puts on her right hand; the man is also to give her a gift of some gold or silver coins according to his means. The priest then gives the blessing as set down in the book; after this they enter the church and he begins the Mass. The bride and groom are to carry lighted candles during the Mass and are to make their offering; before the priest says the *Pax Domini* he places the couple beneath a veil, as is customary, and there gives them the nuptial blessing. Finally, the husband receives the gesture of peace and gives it to his wife."[27]

The rites that are noted above precede the wedding Mass: exchange of consent, joining of the right hands (*dexterarum iunctio*), giving of a ring and coins, and transfer of the dowry before witnesses are simply the traditional rites of betrothal which have now been turned into the Roman Rite. Originally, the priest's role would have been to ensure that there was freedom of consent, that the bride's parents weren't forcing the groom's consent. He also functioned in place of the girl's father in the *traditio puellae* (handing over of the girl, which was also the moment of the joining of the right hands). It was at this moment that the formula *Ego coniungo vos* ("I join you together") was used, or other equivalent formulas.

In Spain and France, there was the blessing of the spouses in the bridal chamber. Over time, this became a blessing of the bridal chamber itself. In France, this blessing of the bridal chamber continued into the nineteenth century.

Although the consent of the spouses—which was juridical in nature—was always regarded as the essence of Marriage for the West, eventually the blessing by the priest likewise came to be required.

---

27 Original Latin text in Dom Edmond Martène, *De antiquis ritibus Ecclesiae*, M 692. English translation taken from A.G. Martimort, *The Church at Prayer: III. The Sacraments*, p. 199.

With regard to the rings, initially the ritual involved the giving of a single ring from groom to bride which symbolized that both were bound to fidelity. By the early tenth century the mutuality of the single ring was being questioned and in Germany rings were given by each of the spouses.[28] The rings came to be understood as having a reference to the covenant, although neither the blessing formula nor the exchange formula made any reference to covenant theology or the Christ/Church spousal imagery. In the Roman ritual of 1614, there was still foreseen only the giving of one ring, though local variation was allowed and encouraged.

A record of the dowry was required as proof of conjugal affection. Ritually speaking, the dowry was symbolized by the monetary gift of a few coins as the groom was able. Evidence of the consent was also given in the record, which came to be called the *Tabellae nuptiales* and was the proof of the existence of the Marriage.

The Council of Trent required that Marriage be celebrated before a priest in order for it to be valid, and the formula *Ego coniungo vos* becomes the quasiform of the sacrament almost equivalent to *Ego te baptizo* (I baptize you) or *Ego te absolvo* (I absolve you). The rite of 1614 laid great emphasis on the priest's role. The spouses answered only "yes" to the priest's questions, which are followed by his joining their hands with the formula and a sprinkling with holy water. Next came the blessing of the ring which the groom placed on the bride's ring finger. There followed some psalm verses and a concluding prayer, and then Mass was celebrated, with the Nuptial Blessing after the Our Father. Before the Tridentine rite (the *Missale Romanum* of 1740), the prayers for the wedding Mass were usually taken from the Mass of the Trinity in order

The wedding liturgy is a pattern for Christian lives.

to show that the love between the divine Persons was the archetype for spousal love. Liturgical reforms following the Council of Trent, however, reclaimed the proper texts for a nuptial Mass from the twelfth century Roman Pontifical.[29]

---

28 See *Handbook for Liturgical Studies*, vol. 4, *Sacraments and Sacramentals*, ed. Anscar J. Chupungco (Collegeville, MN: Liturgical Press, 2000), p. 294.

29 See Mark Searle and Kenneth W. Stevenson, *Documents of the Marriage Liturgy* (Collegeville, MN: The Liturgical Press, 1992), p. 180.

The Council of Trent went out of its way to stress in the Marriage rite its desire that local variations be encouraged and maintained.

Second Vatican Council

Following the Second Vatican Council, Rome promulgated a new Latin typical edition for the *Rite of Marriage* in 1969, which was translated and published in English in 1970. The Congregation for Divine Worship and the Discipline of the Sacraments revised the 1969 edition and promulgated a second typical edition in Latin in 1991. The English translation of the second edition, now known as *The Order of Celebrating Matrimony,* was approved by the Holy See in 2015. This translation has come both because of the revision of the Latin and because of the new translation

A pre-Conciliar wedding liturgy taking place on October 18, 1958 at St. Procopius Parish, New Salem, PA.

principles set forth in the 2001 document *Liturgiam authenticam*. The final approved texts were able to be used on September 8, 2016, and were mandated for liturgical use on December 31, 2016.

The Second Vatican Council took the teaching about local variation straight from the Council of Trent and carried it forward, at least in theory. The *praenotanda* strongly encourages adaptation and inculturation by the local Episcopal Conferences, though this potential seems somewhat under-utilized. Great emphasis is given to the preparation of the celebration, which should involve the couple themselves along with the priest or deacon and those who assist with the celebration, such as the pastoral musician.[30]

These additional changes have been made to the ritual text:

1. There is a large selection of Scripture provided from which to choose:[31]

   - Nine Old Testament Readings
   - Seven Responsorial Psalms
   - Fourteen New Testament Readings
   - Ten Gospel Readings

---

30 The process of preparation will be covered in more detail beginning on page 18.
31 See footnote 56 on page 38.

2. The translation of the psalms is from the *Revised Grail*.

3. There is an additional acclamation and hymn during the Celebration of Matrimony.

4. The formula for the consent is more explicit and there are two forms given.

5. The ancient Preface from the *Old Gelasian Sacramentary* has been restored as an option.

> Thus the man and woman, who "are no longer two but one" (Matthew 19:6), help and serve each other by their marriage partnership; they become conscious of their unity and experience it more deeply from day to day. The intimate union of marriage, as a mutual giving of two persons, and the good of the children demand total fidelity from the spouses and require an unbreakable unity between them.
>
> —*Gaudium et spes*, 48

6. The Nuptial Blessing is now for both spouses, not just the wife, and there are three options provided. It is a compromise, however, as there was some contention about whether to keep the blessing primarily directed toward the wife, in keeping with ancient custom. As a result, part of the prayer is directed solely to the woman, and the rest to them both. It seems unfortunate that this blessing names "the woman an inseparable helpmate to the man,"[32] instead of naming the two as inseparable helpmates for each other, especially when the Council document *Gaudium et spes* emphasizes the mutuality of the couple.[33]

7. An epiclesis has been added to the Nuptial Blessing asking the Father to send the Spirit upon the spouses. These were already published in the third edition of *The Roman Missal*.[34]

8. Cultural adaptations have been added (*arras*, *lazo*, veil).

9. The ritual book includes a revised translation of the Order of Blessing an Engaged Couple and the Order of Blessing a Married Couple within Mass on the Anniversary of Marriage.[35]

---

32 OCM, 74.
33 See GS, 48.
34 See page 53.
35 Additional nuances and changes are addressed in the next chapter.

The latest revision also includes an expanded *praenotanda* or introduction to the ritual.[36] Greater emphasis on the meaning and significance of the sacrament is offered, as is a new emphasis on pastoral preparation and pastoral care for the couple preparing for Marriage. In particular, it is suggested that Catholics who have not received the Sacrament of Confirmation should do so prior to the Celebration of Matrimony "if this can be done without grave inconvenience."[37] In this case one should consider whether there is adequate time to offer appropriate catechesis and formation for Confirmation or whether there will be an opportunity for the celebration of the sacrament with the bishop in a timely fashion without forcing an otherwise unnecessary delay of the Marriage. Pastors are charged with welcoming engaged couples and to "foster and nourish their faith."[38]

> Christian marriages thus enliven society by their witness of fraternity, their social concern, their outspokenness on behalf of the underprivileged, their luminous faith and their active hope. Their fruitfulness expands and in countless ways makes God's love present in society.
>
> — *Amoris laetitia*, 184

The pastoral introduction offers far more information about the duties and ministries of the celebration of the sacrament as well as the preparation for the celebration itself, providing a much more solid foundation of the Celebration of Matrimony as a liturgical act that has a particular place in the life of the whole Church, and not just in the life of the couple. The liturgy of the Church should be seen as a pattern for living out Christian lives. The marital liturgy has come to us today over the course of nearly two thousand years, expressing local customs and proclaiming a Christian marital spirituality. In part, precisely because *The Order of Celebrating Matrimony* maintains its character still today as a domestic reality, it also serves as witness and challenge for all Christian families to live what they celebrate in the liturgy, that is, to become the domestic Church themselves.[39]

---

36 The *praenotanda* was expanded from 18 to 44 articles and includes "The Importance and Dignity of the Sacrament of Matrimony" (1–11); "Duties and Ministries" (12–27); "The Preparation" (28–32); "The Rite to Be Used" (33–38); and "Adaptations to Be Prepared by the Conferences of Bishops" (49–44).

37 OCM, 18.

38 OCM, 16.

39 See *Lumen gentium* (LG), 11.

Preparing the Celebration
of Matrimony

"This is a great mystery, but I speak in reference to Christ and the church.
In any case, each one of you should love his wife as himself,
and the wife should respect her husband."

—Ephesians 5:32–33

St. Paul speaks of Christian Marriage as a "great mystery,"[1] because the union of husband and wife reflects Christ's sacrificial love for his bride, the Church, and the respectful obedience of the Church back to Christ. This quotation comes from one of the options for the Second Reading for the Celebration of Matrimony (although one that is rarely chosen today due to cultural influences), because it expresses clearly the importance of Marriage for the life of the Church. St. Paul is teaching that Christian Marriage is, by nature, a sacrament, because it symbolizes the love of Christ for his bride, the Church. A thorough understanding of the function of Marriage in the life of the Church, and not merely for the life of the married couple themselves, is a good starting point in preparing for the celebration of the Marriage liturgy, because it presumes that the celebration involves the Church because it effects the Church.

Marriage and the Sunday Liturgy

The Sacred Liturgy is "the source and the summit of the Christian life."[2] It is the Sunday Eucharist, the gathering of the parish community to celebrate the Lord's Day, which is the centerpiece of the life of the parish. Marriage, too, is part of the liturgy, as all the sacraments are, and so Marriage is part of the "source and the summit," and it is therefore connected to the Sunday Eucharist. The sacraments are always connected to the community, particularly the parish community, even when they are celebrated apart from the parish. At the Celebration of Matrimony, the gathered assembly may not

---

1 Ephesians 5:32.
2 LG, 11; see also CSL, 10.

be that of the parish community but a particular gathering of the faithful, of family and friends of those to be married, some of whom might not be members of the Catholic faith. The Church is present even in such a limited or exclusive (that is, by invitation) gathering.

The introduction (*praenotanda*) to the second edition of *The Order of Celebrating Matrimony* speaks of the role of the community at wedding lit-

> The liturgy is the summit toward which the activity of the Church is directed; at the same time it is the fount from which all the Church's power flows.
>
> —*Constitution on the Sacred Liturgy,* 10

urgies, which is a helpful addition to the introductory material. Marriage depends on the support of the community, and the gathered assembly—indeed the whole parish community—is enriched by the witness of the couple. It is important to remember this in preparing the Marriage liturgy with the couple who plans to gather their families and friends, but it also opens up other possible settings for the celebration:

"Since Marriage is ordered toward the increase and sanctification of the People of God, its celebration displays a communitarian character that encourages the participation also of the parish community, at least through some of its members. With due regard for local customs and as occasion suggests, several Marriages may be celebrated at the same

Marriage depends on the support of the community and the gathered assembly. Seen here is a wedding at Sunday Mass.

time or the celebration of the Sacrament may take place during the Sunday assembly."[3]

While it might not be practical or in accordance with established customs in many parishes to consider the Sunday liturgy as the setting for the Celebration of Matrimony, doing so is a strong reminder of the importance of the gathered assembly at a wedding and its participation in the liturgical

---

3 OCM, 28.

act. Even the most active and faithful members of parishes occasionally get distracted by the ceremony, the gathering of family and friends, and the emotions, losing sight of what it means to be drawn into "full, conscious, and active participation"[4] in the liturgy itself: to join the couple in praising God for the gift of married love, to pray with and for them for God's grace to strengthen their love and fidelity, and together with the newly married couple to offer themselves in sacrifice along with gifts of bread and wine in the Eucharist. Catechesis, not only for the couple but for the liturgical assembly, is essential, as is an invitation for the assembly to participate in the liturgical act and in the mystery being celebrated rather than merely to witness the Marriage as spectators.

> The Church earnestly desires that all the faithful be led to that full, conscious, and active participation in liturgical celebrations called for by the very nature of the liturgy. Such participation by the Christian people as 'a chosen race, a royal priesthood, a holy nation, God's own people' (1 Peter 2:9, see 2:4–5) is their right and duty by reason of their baptism.
>
> —*Constitution on the Sacred Liturgy*, 14

Celebrating Marriage at a regularly-scheduled parish Sunday Mass could be an effective reminder to both the couple and the community of the importance of married life within the Church. However, this requires attention to what the liturgical norms permit (for example, the use of the Nuptial Mass propers rather than those of the Mass of the day) and a proper balance between the needs of the Sunday assembly and those of the couple and their family and friends gathered. This setting for the Celebration of Matrimony makes good sense if the couple is truly a part of the community; a couple without a real connection to the parish would likely resist such a suggestion. In such a celebration, the couple should still be seated in a prominent place, but the liturgy itself should maintain the look and feel of the Sunday liturgy even when it also includes the couple and their witnesses (for example, the inclusion of the couple with the liturgical ministers in the Entrance Procession).

The Liturgical Year

All liturgical prayer—the sacraments and other rites as well as the Liturgy of the Hours—is set in a particular liturgical time or season. Some liturgical

---

4 CSL, 14.

times have a greater influence on the shape and feel of the rituals than others. The Celebration of Matrimony is no different. Marriage celebrated during Lent, for instance, will take on some of the rubrics and customs of the season, such as omission of the Alleluia before the Gospel (replaced by an appropriate Lenten acclamation[5]) and the more judicious use of flowers.[6] Because of these limitations, some parishes choose not to permit the Celebration of Matrimony during Lent or even Advent, although there is no such restriction per se in liturgical norms. During Easter Time, music during a Nuptial Mass could draw from the repertoire of Easter. The celebration of the Nuptial Mass is governed by the norms laid down in the *General Instruction of the Roman Missal* regarding the use of Ritual Masses.[7] On days when ritual Masses are not permitted, [8] Marriage may be celebrated using the Mass of the Day with its own readings, and the Nuptial Blessing and one of the proper formulae of the Solemn Blessing from *The Order of Celebrating Matrimony* may be included. If the Celebration of Matrimony takes place without Mass, the readings may be taken from *The Order of Celebrating Matrimony*.

> Throughout the course of the year the Church unfolds the entire mystery of Christ.
>
> —*Universal Norms on the Liturgical Year and the General Roman Calendar*, 1

Ministries

The function of the one who presides over the liturgical celebration, at least in regard to the Sacrament of Matrimony, is the officiant and official witness of the Church and the state. It is the spouses themselves who are ministers of the sacrament, in the strict sense of the word, as they give themselves to each other in Marriage; they are the ones who marry each other, as articulated in *Catechism of the Catholic Church*: "According to the Latin tradition,

---

5 A new acclamation and verse for Lenten weddings has been added to *The Order of Celebrating Matrimony;* see OCM, 56 ("Sing joyfully to God our strength" [Psalm 81]).

6 "If a Marriage is celebrated on a day having a penitential character, especially during Lent, the pastor is to counsel the spouses to take into account the special nature of that day" (OCM, 32).

7 "Ritual Masses are connected to the celebration of certain Sacraments or Sacramentals. They are prohibited on Sundays of Advent, Lent, and Easter, on Solemnities, on the days within the Octave of Easter, on the Commemoration of All the Faithful Departed (All Souls' Day), on Ash Wednesday, and during Holy Week, and furthermore due regard is to be had for the norms set out in the ritual books or in the Masses themselves" (*General Instruction of the Roman Missal,* [GIRM], 372); see also OCM, 32: "The celebration of Marriage on Friday of the Passion of the Lord and Holy Saturday is to be avoided altogether."

8 This is outlined in the Table of Liturgical Days as found at the end of *Universal Norms on the Liturgical Year and the General Roman Calendar*.

the spouses as ministers of Christ's grace mutually confer upon each other the sacrament of Matrimony by expressing their consent before the Church."[9] It is obviously the function of a priest (or a bishop) to preside over the Eucharist, and in the context of the Nuptial Mass it is the priest or bishop who presides over the Eucharist and officiates at the Celebration of Matrimony. The ritual text suggests that the priest who prepares the couple for the sacrament ought to be the one who celebrates the Mass, gives the homily, and receives the consent of the couple (presiding over the Marriage Rite).[10]

A deacon may, upon receiving the faculty of the pastor or the local Ordinary, officiate at the Celebration of Matrimony that takes place outside Mass, as indicated in the second and third forms of the rite.[11] Many deacons, along with their wives, participate in the various formation programs for engaged couples, so it is fitting that deacons would also share in this particular function, not only because pastoral circumstances would necessitate their service in this way, but because of the witness that deacons provide as married men. At the same time, one must consider that the Celebration of Matrimony (at least when it is celebrated between two Catholics) rightfully takes place during Mass because of the significance of the newly married couple's participation in the Eucharist as their first act of married life. In this case a couple should not be encouraged to choose to celebrate Marriage outside Mass solely in order to accommodate the service of a deacon as the officiant at the Marriage.

There are also cases in which a couple might invite a priest to celebrate the Mass but wish to ask a deacon to participate as the officiant at the Marriage (to preside over the Celebration of Matrimony within the liturgy as the one who receives the consent of the couple). While a couple might have good intentions for this desire, it is in general not appropriate to mix roles this way, and the ritual text does not forsee such an arrangement. The deacon's role in the Eucharist is to assist the priest, not to preside in his place

---

While the celebration of marriage concerns the spouses and their families, it is not only a private matter. Since their consent is given in the presence of the Church, the celebration of marriage is governed by the appropriate liturgical norms.

—*Sing to the Lord: Music in Divine Worship*, 217

---

9 CCC, 1623.
10 See OCM, 23.
11 See OCM, 24.

GUIDE FOR CELEBRATING® MATRIMONY

at Mass. While the Bishop may make an exception to this general rule, such as when a deacon is asked to witness the consent of one of his children, there are other ways for the deacon to participate in such a wedding, such as giving the homily.

As a liturgical celebration, the Celebration of Matrimony is subject to the norms of the liturgy and the customs of the parish. The participation of liturgical ministers such as servers, readers, and extraordinary ministers of Holy Communion, as they would normally do at Sunday Mass, will help assure the good order and dignity of the liturgy. When couples invite friends or members of their families to fulfill these roles, the parish needs to provide adequate training for those who might not be familiar with local customs, procedures, or the liturgical space. At the very least, it will be helpful to suggest that those who are serving in these roles participate in the wedding rehearsal.

Parishes should provide adequate training for family and friends who serve in liturgical roles at weddings.

Liturgical Music

Music at weddings is often one of the few elements that couples have already thought about before the preparation process begins, but frequently such preconceived notions or expectations are not in keeping with established liturgical norms.

Sing to the Lord: Music in Divine Worship, the guidelines on liturgical music approved by the United States Conference of Catholic Bishops in 2007, states the following in regard to music at weddings:

> Songs that are chosen for the Liturgy should be appropriate for the celebration and express the faith of the Church.[*]
>
> —*Sing to the Lord: Music in Divine Worship*, 220
>
> * See *The Roman Missal*, 30; CSL, 118, 121.

"Particular decisions about the choice and placement of wedding music should be based on the three judgments . . . the liturgical judgment, the pastoral judgment, and the musical judgment. . . . All three of these judgments must be taken into account, since they are aspects of a single judgment. Additionally, music should reflect the truth that all the sacraments celebrate the Paschal Mystery of Christ.* Secular music, even though it may emphasize the love of the spouses for one another, is not appropriate for the Sacred Liturgy. Songs that are chosen for the Liturgy should be appropriate for the celebration and express the faith of the Church.**"[12]

Couples might not understand the values of the musical, liturgical, and pastoral judgments, so they might need to be guided in this regard. *Sing to the Lord* advises, "Since oftentimes the only music familiar to the couple is not necessarily suitable to the sacrament, the pastoral musician will make an effort to demonstrate a wide range of music appropriate for the Liturgy."[13]

A trained cantor is necessary to lead the assembly in song at weddings.

Because the Marriage ritual is above all a liturgical act, music for the liturgy is primarily about praise and thanks to God, particularly for the gift of the grace of the sacrament, the blessing of families and friends, and for married love which mirrors God's love. Priority should be given to those parts such as responses, acclamations, and other ritual texts that are normally sung by the assembly. In order to facilitate the participation of the assembly, preparation of a helpful worship aid[14] is important, as is the ministry of a trained cantor—not merely a soloist—who is familiar with the parish repertoire of responses and acclamations and is experienced at leading the assembly in song.[15]

The Order of Celebrating Matrimony includes chant settings of the Nuptial Blessing, which are found in chapter IV, part VII, Other Prayers of Nuptial Blessing. If the Nuptial Blessing is to be chanted, presiders should rehearse technique, cadence, and flow with the parish music director. The music director may also provide a recording of the chant settings for the

---

12 *Sing to the Lord: Music in Divine Worship* (STL), 220; *see CSL , 61; CCC , 1621; ** see *The Roman Missal*, 30; CSL, 118, 121.

13 STL, 218.

14 See STL, 224.

15 Particular musical considerations for the various parts of the liturgy will be addressed in each section beginning on page 29.

presider to use for rehearsal purposes.[16] A competent musician will be able to provide accompaniment for the presider if it is needed during the liturgy; although the chants are meant to be unaccompanied.

The Liturgical Environment

The Order of Celebrating Matrimony says very little about the liturgical space, the arrangement of furnishings, and the decoration or adornment of the space, in part because the variations of the different forms of architecture and design of individual churches cannot be taken into consideration in the rubrics and introductory material.

The Rite of Christian Marriage contains no directives about the spatial requirements for the celebration. Instead, the ritual focuses upon the consent given by the bride and the groom, the ambo from which the word of God is proclaimed, and the altar at which the couple share the Body and Blood of Christ within a nuptial Mass.

—*Built of Living Stones: Art, Architecture, and Worship*, 106

In many parishes it is the custom to have the bride and groom (and perhaps their principal witnesses) seated in the sanctuary.[17] As ministers of the sacrament and a living sign of Christ's love for his bride, the Church, the groom and bride are together a witness, and they ought to be visible to the gathered assembly. The design of churches and any subsequent renovation of sanctuaries or worship spaces ought to take into consideration the needs of the various liturgical rites to be celebrated there, including Marriage.[18]

Flowers or other decorations provided either by the couple or by the parish must be in harmony with the design of the liturgical space, sensitive to the primary furnishings of the sanctuary (the altar, the ambo, the chair, and the tabernacle), and in keeping with the norms of the liturgical season. During Easter Time, for example, the couple should be made aware of the flowers and other decorations that are already present so as not to contradict what is in place or "clutter it" with too many floral arrangements. During Advent and Lent, couples should be sensitive to the liturgical norms and the call for restraint regarding the use of flowers. Flowers "should always show

---

16 Recordings for training purposes are available from the National Association of Pastoral Ministers' website (www.NPM.org).

17 See also page 27.

18 See *Built of Living Stones: Art, Architecture, and Worship* (BLS), 107 and 108.

moderation and be arranged around the altar rather than on the altar table."[19] The use of flowers as a memorial tribute can be a subtle but effective means of remembering family members or friends of the couple who have died. Their names may be printed in the wedding worship aid. Couples may be encouraged to donate the sanctuary flowers for use at Sunday Mass.

Decorations must be in harmony with the season and the liturgical space.

Discussion of flowers and other decorations for the liturgical space should also include bouquets for the bride and other members of the bridal party as well as the use of a white runner for the aisle, a practice which was once commonplace but has fallen out of practice in recent years. The runner serves no practical purpose and it can in fact create trip hazards for those who walk in the procession as well as for those who participate in the Communion Procession.

Vesture for liturgical ministers is an essential part of the liturgical environment, for it communicates a sense of dignity and sacredness of the ritual action taking place. It also serves as a visual "cue" of the connection of the Celebration of Matrimony to the rest of the liturgical life of the Church. For a Nuptial Mass the sacred vesture for the priest celebrant is the vesture prescribed for Mass: the stole and chasuble. The solemnity of the occasion of a Ritual Mass suggests that among white vestments the more festive vesture could be used (unless the Marriage takes place on a Sunday or other solemnity, in which case the color of the day is worn). If a deacon is assisting he should be vested in a dalmatic. Those assisting as servers should be vested in the customary vesture of servers for the parish, and if it is the custom of the parish for other ministers such as cantors, readers, or extraordinary ministers to be vested (such as wearing an alb), then consideration should be given to following that custom even for a Nuptial Mass.

For the Celebration of Matrimony Without Mass, a priest could vest in a cope and stole over an alb or over a cassock and surplice, or just a stole over the alb or cassock and surplice.[20] According to the rubrics, a deacon officiat-

---

19 GIRM, 305.
20 See OCM, 83; see also OCM, 45 and 48 regarding the priest's vesture at Mass.

GUIDE FOR CELEBRATING® MATRIMONY

ing at Marriage without Mass wears a stole and dalmatic over an alb or just a stole over the alb.[21]

It is a pastoral gesture to couples to use the parish's finer vestments, linens, and vessels for this celebration, giving yet another indication of the solemnity and dignity of the rite.

The Arrangement of the Bridal Party

The arrangement of ministers, the bride and groom, their witnesses, and the bridal party is dictated by the norms of the liturgy, the configuration of the sanctuary and the church, and the particular situation and configuration of the bridal party. While it is impossible to foresee every possible scenario, some general observations may be helpful. One must keep in mind and respect the design of the liturgical space and the primary elements therein: the altar, the ambo (pulpit), the place for the celebrant, the tabernacle or place of reservation of the Eucharist, and the baptismal font or baptistery. In the Celebration of Matrimony, a prominent place should be provided for the couple, for they themselves are the living sign in the Sacrament of Matrimony. Still, that place of prominence must respect the other elements, especially when Marriage is celebrated during Mass, for their place should not obscure the liturgical assembly's ability to see and to participate in the liturgical actions taking place. For instance, a large number of attendants in a bridal party would be better accommodated within the front part of the assembly rather than in the sanctuary.

Paul Turner states:

> "In the popular imagination, a wedding takes place in a church with a bride and groom kneeling together in front of the altar. This arrangement is not mentioned in *The Order of Celebrating Matrimony*. Instead, the rite gives the couple the option of kneeling at their place for the Nuptial Blessing. Alternatively, they may approach the altar and stand for the blessing.
>
> "The bride and groom are members of the assembly, and they should take the posture everyone else does. That means they should be able to sit for most of the Liturgy of the Word. If the wedding includes Mass, they should kneel when others kneel. The couple disrupts the unity of the assembly if they kneel while others sit. Many couples take their place at a kneeler facing the back wall. But they could take seats in the sanctuary facing out.

---

21 See OCM, 83.

During the exchange of consent, some priests position themselves between the couple and the rest of the assembly. When the bride and groom turn to him, everyone else sees their faces, too. If the wedding takes place apart from Mass, the liturgy never requires anyone to kneel. But there are times for standing and sitting. Some brides don't want to sit because of their dress. Let them know early on that they will be invited to sit for part of the ceremony. The dress should accommodate itself to the liturgy; the liturgy need not accommodate itself to the dress."[22]

During the Celebration of Matrimony, as has been observed already, the bride and the groom are the ministers of the sacrament, and the priest or deacon acts as the officiant and primary witness. How this is arranged will depend on the configuration of the sanctuary, but the couple should be clearly visible to the assembly, and when they make their vows to each other, accommodations should be made so that they can be heard.

The Order of Celebrating Matrimony: Three Forms of the Rite

The Order of Celebrating Matrimony includes three different forms of the rite:
- The Order of Celebrating Matrimony within Mass (chapter I)
- The Order of Celebrating Matrimony without Mass (chapter II)
- The Order of Celebrating Matrimony between a Catholic and a Catechumen or a Non-Christian (chapter III)[23]

When two Catholics marry, the celebration normally takes place within Mass in order that the couple may be nourished and strengthened by the Eucharist as they begin their married life together. As mentioned before, every liturgy is a celebration of the Lord's Paschal Mystery, of the whole of the ministry, Passion, Death, and Resurrection of the Lord. Marriage is a unique expression of the Paschal Mystery, as the spouses die to themselves

---

22 Paul Turner, "Preparing the Wedding Liturgy," *Pastoral Liturgy*® 40, no. 3 (May/June 2009).

23 A fourth form of the rite, "The Order of Celebrating Matrimony before an Assisting Layperson," found in the Latin *editio typical altera* ("second typical edition"), was not included in the English translation of the second edition of the Marriage Rite for use in the dioceses of the United States of America, and will therefore not be addressed in this study. Chapter IV of the OCM includes Various Texts to Be Used in the Rite of Marriage and in the Mass for the Celebration of Marriage. This includes additional Scripture texts and orations. The OCM also includes an appendix. Part I of the appendix includes sample texts for the Universal Prayer; part II includes the Order of Blessing an Engaged Couple; and part III includes the Order of Blessing a Married Couple within Mass on the Anniversary of Marriage.

in order to live for each other; this is their vocation. Marriage is sacrificial, an offering of the self, and that offering of self is then ritualized in the offering of self together with the gifts of the Eucharist. Furthermore, the Eucharist as a sacrifice of praise and thanksgiving becomes the first act of the newly married couple as they stand together before the Lord. The Eucharist, in a certain sense, seals their commitment.

Marriage between a Catholic and a baptized Christian of another confession (denomination) normally takes place without Mass, although for pastoral reasons and with permission of the local ordinary, the rite for celebrating within Mass may be used.[24] The ritual text cautions that the norms for admission to Communion for those who are not Catholic should be followed. Therefore, celebrating Marriage in these cases within Mass ought not to be encouraged, as the celebration of the Eucharist would immediately bring to light a division between the spouses rather than signify their union as husband and wife, as one of whom would not lawfully be able to share in Communion.[25]

The third form of the celebration is for use at marriages between a Catholic and a catechumen or a non-Christian (an unbaptized person). By definition such a marriage is not sacramental—although it is lawful, valid, and permanent—for an unbaptized person cannot enter into a sacrament. Many texts are adapted to fit the unique situation and sensitivities of a spouse who is not Christian and his or her family and friends. A special form of the Nuptial Blessing is provided as well, though the circumstances may suggest that the Nuptial Blessing be omitted, in which case an alternate prayer is offered. Many of the normal greetings are omitted, and the Liturgy of the Word can be adapted with fewer than the normal number of readings.[26]

Celebrating Matrimony within Mass

Introductory Rites

Entrance Procession and Chant

The Entrance Procession is a highly symbolic ritual that has the power to communicate truth about what the Church believes regarding Marriage as the couple comes before Lord to seek the blessing of his grace. It also has the

---

24 See OCM, 36.

25 If both spouses are Catholic and the majority of their guests are not Catholic, this would also be a legitimate pastoral reason to celebrate the Marriage without Mass.

26 See also page 61.

The bride and groom may process separately and accompanied by both their parents.

power to draw the liturgical assembly into an act of worship rather than merely to set the stage for the assembly to act as spectators. The procession of the ministers, the bridal party, and the couple can take on many forms, but those forms must be derived from one of the two forms of entrance which are described in the rubrics of the liturgical text.[27]

The ritual text describes two forms of the Entrance Procession. The first involves a procession that may include the liturgical ministers, and takes place after the priest (or deacon in the case of a celebration outside Mass) receives the couple at the door. The second involves a procession of the bridal party who are then received at the altar by the priest (or deacon).[28]

The First Form

At the appointed time, the Priest, wearing an alb and a stole and chasuble of the color of the Mass to be celebrated, goes with the servers to the door of the church, receives the bridal party, and warmly greets them, showing that the Church shares in their joy.

The procession to the altar then takes place in the customary manner. Meanwhile, the Entrance Chant takes place.

The Priest approaches the altar, reverences it with a profound bow, and venerates it with a kiss. After this, he goes to the chair.[29]

The Second Form

At the appointed time, the Priest, wearing an alb and a stole and chasuble of the color of the Mass to be celebrated, goes with the servers to the place prepared for the couple or to his chair.

When the couple have arrived at their place, the Priest receives them and warmly greets them, showing that the Church shares in their joy.

---

27 See OCM, 45–50.

28 Notice that in the second form, the rubrics note that the priest greets the couple after they have arrived at their place. This presumes that the *couple* processes to the place where they will be seated rather than the groom coming from the side with his best man and groomsmen.

29 OCM, 45–47.

Then, during the Entrance Chant, the Priest approaches the altar, reverences it with a profound bow, and venerates it with a kiss. After this, he goes to the chair.[30]

Most couples, especially brides, come with preconceived notions of what the Entrance Procession should look like, and many of their expectations are formed not from experiences of the liturgy but from what they have seen or experienced, either as members of bridal parties at other weddings, at weddings in secular contexts, or in other religious settings without the ritual framework that is part of Roman Catholic liturgy. The first form of the entrance states only that "the procession to the altar takes place in the customary manner." "Customary" could refer to the typical way in which any Mass begins with a procession of those serving in liturgical roles. It could also refer to the variety of customs that are observed at the Celebration of Matrimony. The 1969 edition of the *Rite of Marriage* stated this:

The bride and groom may process as a couple.

> If there is a procession to the altar, the <u>ministers go first</u>, <u>followed by the priest</u>, and <u>then the bride and groom</u>. According to <u>local custom</u>, they may be escorted by at least <u>their parents and the two witnesses</u>. Meanwhile, the entrance song is sung.[31]

Early drafts of the *Odo Celebrandi Matrimonium, editio typica altera,* included a similar description of the Entrance Procession. This description is even included in the Spanish translation of the ritual for use in the Dioceses of the United States.[32] The 2016 English translation of the second edition of the Latin ritual simplified the rubric regarding the procession, but it would seem that "customary manner" could correctly refer to the description found in the earlier edition.

---

30 OCM, 48–50.

31 *Rite of Marriage* (1969), 20 (the underlined text refers to the Spanish comparison in footnote 32).

32 See *Ritual del Matrimonio*, 46 (the phrases that are underlined correspond to the rubric from the 1969 English translation concerning order of procession and those involved): "Luego se hace la procession hacia el altar: <u>preceden los ayudantes</u>, <u>sigue el sacerdote</u>, <u>después los novios</u>, a los que, según <u>las costumbres locales</u>, pueden acompañar honoríficamente, por lo menos <u>los padres y dos testigos</u>, hasta el lugar que tienen preparado. Mientras, se entona el canto de endtrada."

One of the significant challenges to enacting the procession in the spirit of the ritual text is the cultural custom (or superstition) of the bride and groom remaining separated from one another until they arrive at the altar. This custom was rooted in a tradition of arranged marriages in which the groom did not see the bride until they were face-to-face at the altar. The bride was hidden before the start of the ceremony, and was veiled until her father presented her to the groom. Even though the current cultural climate is far removed from this experience, the custom of the bride and groom "not seeing one another" is a strongly-held value for many couples.

The entrance procession should not be focused entirely on the bride and her attendants.

The participation of parents in the Entrance Procession can be a sensitive issue as well. A common arrangement of the Entrance Procession focuses solely on the bride and her attendants who enter in a solemn procession, while the liturgical ministers and the groom and his attendants appear in the sanctuary either directly from the sacristy, or worse yet, form their own procession down a side aisle. This custom is reinforced by weddings depicted on television and in movies, which does not reflect a sophisticated liturgical vision of the Celebration of Matrimony. This practice likely flows from ancient traditions in which the bride was presented by her father to the man chosen by prearrangement to be the husband.[33] More often than not, couples presume that the father of the bride will escort or "give away" the bride in the Entrance Procession, while the bride's mother and the groom's parents will already be seated prior to the Entrance Procession. This custom, too, is rooted in a tradition of arranged marriages. Clearly such an arrangement is not the case today, yet this arrangement places all the focus on the bride alone in the entrance procession, preceded by her attendants and escorted or "given away" by her father, which harkens to a time of marriages arranged by the parents of the bride and groom. If Marriage is an equal partnership between spouses, both of whom enter freely into the Marriage covenant, then the Entrance Procession ought to reflect that reality. Today the participation of parents represents their support for their son or daughter as they enter into Marriage and the example they have given as a witness to

33 See the first chapter, "The Theological and Historical Developments of the Catholic Marriage Ritual."

married life. For this reason the arrangement of the procession as described in *The Order of Celebrating Matrimony*, and described above, is a much more effective ritual as it reflects the lived experience of the spouses. Great sensitivity must be shown in conversations with couples in regard to their expectations and to unique family situations. For many reasons it would be helpful to discuss with a couple what they have learned about Marriage and family life, for better or worse, from their own families.

Since both forms of the entrance described in the ritual text are somewhat vague and allow for the influence of local custom as well as the particular arrangement of the liturgical space (the entrance or gathering space as well as the sanctuary), it is possible to harmonize expectations of couples with the principles of the liturgy.

Here is one possible configuration (in order of first to last), making use of the first form of the procession:

The witnesses and other attendants may process together.

servers with processional cross and candles (and even incense)

deacon or reader bearing the *Book of the Gospels*

priest

groom's attendants

best man

groom, escorted by parents

bride's attendants

maid/matron of honor

bride, escorted by parents (or father)

An alternative form is this arrangement:

servers with processional cross and candles (and even incense)

deacon or reader bearing the *Book of the Gospels*

priest

groom's attendants together with bride's attendants

groom's parents

bride's parents

best man and maid/matron of honor

bride and groom

Both forms of the Entrance Procession mention the Entrance Chant. What is sung at the entrance follows the norms laid out in the *General Instruction of the Roman Missal*.[34] The proper Entrance Antiphons from *The Roman Missal* are included in the three Ritual Masses for the Celebration of Matrimony:

Option A

May the Lord send you help from the holy place
and give you support from Sion.
May he grant you your hearts' desire
and fulfill every one of your designs.[35]

Option B

At dawn, O Lord, fill us with your merciful love,
and we shall exult and rejoice all our days.
Let the favor of the Lord our God be upon us
and upon the work of our hands.[36]

Option C

I will bless you day after day, O Lord,
and praise your name for ever and ever,
for you are kind to all
and compassionate to all your creatures.[37]

These texts indicate the intention of expressing praise for God's providential love and care for his people, and seeking God's blessing in a particular way upon the couple. Music ministers should note that an Alleluia may be added to the end of the antiphon during Easter Time. The choice of other chants, hymns, or songs should be inspired by the intentions expressed here, keeping in mind the abilities of the particular gathered assembly.

Since the actual procession of the ministers, the couple, and the bridal party might be a substantial and lengthy procession, instrumental music could be used in addition to what is sung. Given expectations about "traditional" music for wedding processions, one might suggest having an Entrance Antiphon sung or chanted (by the cantor, or by the cantor and the people)

---

34 See GIRM, 48; see also STL, 142–144, and 222.
35 *The Roman Missal*, Ritual Mass for the Celebration of Marriage, A; see Psalm 20 (19):3, 5.
36 *The Roman Missal*, Ritual Mass for the Celebration of Marriage, B; see Psalm 90 (89):14, 17.
37 *The Roman Missal*, Ritual Mass for the Celebration of Marriage, C; see Psalm 145 (144):2, 9.

before the actual procession begins, as a call to worship, or at the end of the actual procession as the couple arrives in the sanctuary. Or, instrumental music may accompany the procession to the sanctuary, at which point an Entrance Hymn or Song is sung. The Entrance Chant, Song, or Hymn may also accompany the procession itself as indicated in the rite.[38]

Reception of the Couple

After the Sign of the Cross, the priest "greets those present, using one of the formulas provided in *The Roman Missal*,"[39] that is, one of the liturgical greetings from the Order of Mass such as "The Lord be with you." The people respond, "And with your spirit." Then "the Priest addresses the couple" and the people to "dispose them inwardly for the celebration of Marriage."[40]

Now included in the ritual text are two sample forms of address for receiving the couple and introducing the liturgy. Since the rubrics of the Order of the Mass suggest that the priest may briefly introduce the Mass of the day or the occasion being celebrated, it has been the custom for many priests to offer words of welcome to the couple and to those gathered as an introductory exhortation. Two sample addresses are included, along with the rubric, "in these or similar words."[41] The first form addresses the assembly about the gathering in the presence of the couple in order to invite their prayerful support and participation in the liturgy:

> We have come rejoicing into the house of the Lord
> for this celebration, dear brothers and sisters,
> and now we stand with **N.** and **N.**
> on the day they intend to form a home of their own.
> For them this is a moment of unique importance.
> So let us support them
> with our affection,
> with our friendship,
> and with our prayer as their brothers and sisters.
> Let us listen attentively with them
> to the word that God speaks to us today.

---

38 The Litany of Saints could even be sung while the Entrance Procession takes place. This is a powerful witness that the entire communion of saints have joined with those present at the liturgy to pray for the couple about to be married.

39 OCM, 51.

40 OCM, 52.

41 OCM, 52.

Then, with holy Church,
let us humbly pray to God the Father,
through Christ our Lord,
for this couple, his servants,
that he lovingly accept them,
bless them,
and make them always one.[42]

The second form addresses the couple directly and allows the celebrant, on behalf of the gathered assembly, to express the hope that the Lord will hear their prayers and be a source of help and guidance in their married life:

N. and N., the Church shares your joy
and warmly welcomes you,
together with your families and friends,
as today,
in the presence of God our Father,
you establish between yourselves
a lifelong partnership.
May the Lord hear you on this your joyful day.
May he send you help from heaven and protect you.
May he grant you your hearts' desire
and fulfill every one of your prayers.[43]

This act of receiving the couple replaces the Penitential Act (as it similarly does at the Rite of Acceptance in to the Order of Catechumens, at the Rite of Baptism for Children when it is celebrated at Mass, or at the reception of the body at the funeral Mass). The omission of the Penitential Act includes the omission of the Kyrie, since the Kyrie is always part of the Penitential Act.

Gloria

The third edition of *The Roman Missal,* introduced late 2011, included a rubric in the Ritual Mass formularies for Marriage prescribing the use of the Gloria within Mass.[44] The *General Instruction of the Roman Missal* states that the Gloria is used "on Sundays outside Advent and Lent, and also on Solemnities and Feasts, and at particular celebrations of a more solemn character."[45] Since

---

42 OCM, 52.
43 OCM, 53.
44 See *The Roman Missal*, Ritual Masses, V. For the Celebration of Marriage (A, B, and C).
45 GIRM, 53.

the Gloria is prescribed for most of the Ritual Masses such as Baptism, Confirmation, Holy Orders, and religious profession, its use within the Celebration of Matrimony is fitting. It does present pastoral challenges, however, since often the particular assembly gathered for a Catholic wedding includes people from outside the parish, those who do not practice their Catholic faith regularly, and often those who are not Catholic. Particular attention should be given to choosing a setting of the Gloria that is easy to learn and sing, perhaps using the chant found in *The Roman Missal* or a setting with a simple refrain rather than a through-composed setting.[46]

In preparing the rite, the priest, liturgist, and the pastoral musician should also be sensitive to the danger of "overloading" the Introductory Rites. Since the Entrance Procession itself can be rather substantial with the participation of a large number of attendants in the bridal party, one might consider whether an Entrance Chant or Song should follow after an instrumental processional, followed by an extended introductory address, and then the Gloria (particularly if the Gloria itself would be lengthened by the use of a refrain). While each of these elements is suggested or, in the case of the Gloria, prescribed, one should strive for a balance so that the Introductory Rites do not overshadow what follows.

Collect

Although it is not specifically noted in *The Order of Celebrating Matrimony*, the Collect concludes the Introductory Rite. Presiders should allow the moment of silent prayer called for by the invitation "Let us pray." The six options for the Collect emphasize the sacramental nature of the marital covenant and ask that the couple "may grow in the faith,"[47] "be kept safe by [God's] assistance,"[48] and that "they may be bound together / in mutual affection, / in likeness of mind, / and in shared holiness."[49] The texts are found in *The Roman Missal*[50] as well as in *The Order of Celebrating Matrimony*, chapter IV, part II, "Collects."[51]

---

46 See STL, 149.

47 OCM, 191.

48 OCM, 192.

49 OCM, 193.

50 See Ritual Masses, V. For the Celebration of Marriage, options A–C.

51 OCM, 188–190. See also OCM, 188, which states that the first option for the Collect ("O God, . . .) who consecrated the bond of Marriage . . . ") is not to be used if the first option for the Nuptial Blessing is chosen (see OCM, 74 and 105).

The Liturgy of the Word

"The Liturgy of the Word is celebrated in the usual manner."[52] Scripture readings are normally taken from those texts provided in *The Order of Celebrating Matrimony* at numbers, 144–187.[53] The *praenotanda* explains the goals of the Liturgy of the Word are to express "the importance of Christian Marriage in the history of salvation and the responsibilities and duties of Marriage to be attended to for the sanctification of the spouses and of their children."[54]

Normally there are three readings (plus the Responsorial Psalm) at the Celebration of Matrimony that takes place within or without Mass. Although at the Celebration of Matrimony between a Catholic and a Catechumen or Non-Christian, the Liturgy of the Word may take place as usual, there is the option that "there may be only one reading."[55] No particular reason is indicated, however, for omitting a reading. If readings are omitted, ideally couples will select an Old Testament reading followed by the Responsorial Psalm and the Gospel. However, pastoral sensitivity to particular ecumenical or interfaith circumstances might warrant proclamation of only one reading, thus, omitting any readings from the New Testament including the Gospel (for example, if a Catholic marries a devout Jewish or Muslim person). Although the psalm could certainly follow the Old Testament reading, this is not necessarily required.

Several readings were added to the options from which to choose, including a Lenten option for the Gospel Acclamation.[56] The new edition of the ritual indicates, "[a]t least one reading that explicitly speaks of Marriage must always be chosen"[57] Presumably this is to assure that the goals of the Liturgy of the Word are addressed in some way. The texts of all the readings are provided in chapter IV of *The Order of Celebrating Matrimony*, and those that

---

52 OCM, 55.

53 These are found in chapter IV, part I of *The Order of Celebrating Matrimony*, "Biblical Readings."

54 OCM, 35.

55 OCM, 122.

56 Additional readings were added to the *Ordo Celebrandi Matrimonium, editio typica altera*—all but Ephesians 4:1–6 were added to the *Lectionary for Mass* when this ritual book was revised in 1998 ("For the Conferral of the Sacrament of Marriage," 801–805). Until future revisions and editions of the Lectionary, those who prepare the liturgy will need to use Lectionary #807.2 if this reading will be read at a wedding (the reading is found in the Ritual Mass for the Blessing of Abbots and Abbesses). Parish staffs should also note the translation of the Psalms that is found in the OCM is from the Grail Psalter. This will differ from the Lectionary which uses a variation of the New American Bible. When the Lectionary is eventually revised, the translation of the psalms will change from the NAB to the Revised Grail.

57 OCM, 55.

explicitly speak of Marriage are marked with an asterisk. The following readings have been designated as such:

- Genesis 1:26–28, 31a
- Genesis 2:18–24
- Genesis 24:48–51, 58–67
- Tobit 7:6–14
- Tobit 8:4b–8
- Proverbs 31:10–13, 19–20, 30–31
- Sirach 26:1–4, 13–16
- Psalm 128:1–2, 3, 4–5ac and 6a
- Ephesians 5:2a, 21–33 (long form) or 5:2a, 25–32 (short form)
- 1 Peter 3:1–9
- Matthew 19:3–6
- Mark 10:6–9
- John 2:1–11

The celebration of the Liturgy of the Word "in the usual manner"[58] includes the use of the proper liturgical books: the *Lectionary for Mass* and the *Book of the Gospels*. To show appropriate reverence for the Word of God one should avoid the use of photocopied pages which a reader removes from his or her pocket. In the cases of the use of those readings which are not included in the present edition of the *Lectionary for Mass*, one might prepare the texts in a dignified binder that could substitute for the Lectionary. The readers should be present at the wedding rehearsal so that they can become familiar with Lectionary or ritual binder, know the logistics for their assigned reading, as well as be given the option to practice reading the texts publically.

Even if not carried in the Entrance Procession, the *Book of the Gospels* could be used by having it placed on the altar prior to the start of the liturgy so that the deacon or priest may process with it to the ambo during the singing of the Gospel Acclamation. If there is an adequate number of servers, a procession with the *Book of Gospels* could also include incense and candles. If a deacon is present, he will usually proclaim the Gospel.

---

58 OCM, 55.

The Homily

In the Celebration of Matrimony, the homily can be a moment of profound impact on the couple and on the gathered assembly, but at the same time preachers face particular challenges to effective preaching on the occasion of a wedding. The rubrics in the ritual text outline the aim of preaching:

> "After the reading of the Gospel, the Priest in the Homily uses the sacred text to expound the mystery of Christian Marriage, the dignity of conjugal love, the grace of the Sacrament, and the responsibilities of married people, keeping in mind, however, the various circumstances of individuals."[59]

Additionally, the rubrics note that at the Celebration of Matrimony between a Catholic and a Catechumen or a Non-Christian, adaptation (not merely "keeping in mind") of the homily to particular circumstances is required: "After this, there should be a homily on the sacred text, which should be adapted to the responsibilities and situation of the couple and other circumstances."[60]

Because the homily is also situated in a liturgical context, it should have the aim of preparing the couple and the assembly to enter into the mystery of the Sacrament of Matrimony, and in the case of the Nuptial Mass, to lead them to the offering of praise and thanksgiving in the Eucharist, as the bishops of the United States point out in *Preaching the Mystery of Faith:*

> "One of the most important teachings of Vatican II in regard to preaching is the insistence that the homily is an integral part of the Eucharist itself.* As part of the entire liturgical act, the homily is meant to set hearts on fire with praise and thanksgiving. It is to be a feature of the intense and privileged encounter with Jesus Christ that takes place in the liturgy. One might even say that the homilist connects the two parts of the Eucharistic liturgy as he looks back at the Scripture readings and looks forward to the sacrificial meal."[61]

While this is speaking primarily about the homily in the Sunday liturgy, it serves as a reminder that the homily is not merely catechetical but liturgical. The preacher cannot expect to offer a complete catechesis on the Sacrament of Matrimony; the homily cannot make up for sacramental preparation and formation that should have taken place in the months prior to the wedding.

---

59 OCM, 57.
60 OCM, 123.
61 *Preaching the Mystery of Faith*, p. 17; *see CSL, 52.

Preaching at weddings, then, should focus not only on teaching about the nature and duties of Marriage, but on thanksgiving and praise for the gifts of married life. Because oftentimes the guests in attendance are not frequent churchgoers, the homily at a wedding can also be a source of evangelization, so it ought to be an encouragement to the couple and to the assembly to live the Gospel and take up their particular vocation. The preacher could highlight the blessing of God's love for us as a source of grace to love one another. In addition, it is helpful to explain how the couple to be married is a witness and an example insofar as they become a sacramental sign of God's love.

The homily at a wedding is an opportunity for evangelization—it ought to encourage the couple and the assembly to live the Gospel.

The *General Instruction of the Roman Missal* states that the homily can be based not only on the Scriptures but on other texts and aspects of the liturgy as well:

> "[The homily] should be an explanation of some aspect of the readings from Sacred Scripture or of another text from the Ordinary or the Proper of the Mass of the day and should take into account both the mystery being celebrated and the particular needs of the listeners."[62]

For pastors who celebrate a large number of weddings in addition to funerals, Sunday, and daily Masses, it might, on occasion, be difficult to craft or prepare an entirely new homily for each and every wedding. Preachers should remember that the homily can be based on the occasion, the nature of the Sacrament of Matrimony, and the ritual texts of the rite as well as the Scripture readings that the couple has chosen. For this reason it might also be helpful to invite the couple to prepare some reflections on the particular readings they have chosen and the reasons for making their particular choices. The preacher can use these reflections as background in order to understand the couple's faith and their own understanding of the mystery being celebrated.

---

62 GIRM, 65.

Preachers often face particular challenges at weddings. There are sometimes great expectations from couples and their families and friends that the mood should be light-hearted or "fun," and that the priest or deacon should merely talk about the couple or be funny. Given the vastly different forms of the celebrations of weddings that many people have experienced, participants may not be ready for a substantial homily, or they may be distracted or preoccupied with other elements of the wedding, such as flowers, dresses, music, or friends and family. There may be particular family situations that could also interfere with effective preaching. For example, a preacher who focuses solely on the notion of the indissolubility of Marriage at a wedding where the parents of the bride or the groom have experienced divorce or remarriage could fall on deaf ears, or draw undue attention to a tense situation. Understanding the couple and their experiences can only help the preacher to be more effective. In the end, the rites themselves ought to speak clearly—signs, symbols, and words are already "preaching." It is the preacher's job to point to those and lead the assembly to experience them more fully.

> Preparation for preaching is so important a task that a prolonged time of study, prayer, reflection and pastoral creativity should be devoted to it.
>
> —*Evangelii gaudium*, 145

Pastoral guidance for the wedding homily can also be found in Pope Francis' apostolic exhortations, *Amoris laetitia: On Love in the Family*[63] and *Evangelii gaudium: On the Proclamation of the Gospel in Today's World*. Pope Francis, both by his example and in his writings, has sought to encourage the importance of the homily as a tool of evangelization, of catechesis, of encouragement, and of spirituality. In order to have "a worthwhile dialogue we have to have something to say. This can only be the fruit of an interior richness nourished by reading, personal reflection, prayer and openness to the world around us."[64] Although Francis is referring to the dialogue between a husband and wife, it certainly applies to the homily for "the liturgical proclamation of the word of God, especially in the Eucharistic assembly, is not so much a time for meditation and catechesis as a dialogue between God and his people."[65] As the primary facilitator of that dialogue, it is necessary for

---

63 See especially EG, 135–159 concerning the homily; see also AL, 205-216 regarding Marriage preparation, and 212–216 regarding the celebration itself.

64 AL, 141.

65 EG, 137; quoting *Dies Domini*, 41.

the preacher "to have something to say."[66] The primary sources for the homily are always first and foremost the proclaimed Word of God, but also human experience, and the liturgical rite itself. *The Order of Celebrating Matrimony*, especially the expanded *praenotanda*, is a treasure trove of insights and wisdom that can be cracked open with the tool of "personal reflection, prayer and openness to the world around."[67]

It seems that a central tenet for Pope Francis regarding the homily is that it becomes a personal encounter within the liturgy. "The Lord truly enjoys talking with his people; the preacher should strive to communicate that same enjoyment to his listeners."[68] In fact, if one were to try to sum up the key for inspired preaching for Pope Francis, it would be that the preacher must find the insight or image that fills himself with joy. Equal to the content communicated is the joy in which it is communicated.

> "The challenge of an inculturated preaching consists in proclaiming a synthesis, not ideas or detached values. Where your synthesis is, there lies your heart. The difference between enlightening people with a synthesis and doing so with detached ideas is like the difference between boredom and heartfelt fervor."[69]

Until the preacher is himself stirred by the message he is preparing, he's not ready to preach it. "It is not great knowledge, but rather the ability to feel and relish things interiorly that contents and satisfies the soul."[70] This is not to say that the homily must be emotionally manipulative, but rather that the challenge for the preacher is to take the scriptural, ritual, and doctrinal insights for the wedding day and find the kernel insight that will raise, inspire, and ennoble the hearts of the bride and groom and whole assembly.

For good or ill, this demands time and preparation. The two greatest impacts that a presider exerts on the assembly are his prayerful presence and his meaning-filled preaching. "It is useless to attempt to read a biblical text if all we are looking for are quick, easy and immediate results. Preparation for preaching requires love."[71] Even in our preaching and in our preparation for preaching, the preacher can witness to the married couple on the virtue of love. And hopefully on the joy of love.

---

66 AL, 141.
67 AL, 141.
68 EG, 141.
69 EG, 143.
70 AL, 207.
71 EG, 146.

The Celebration of Matrimony

The Celebration of Matrimony within Mass takes place after the homily. The main elements are the questions before the consent, in which the couple expresses their freedom of choice, fidelity, and the acceptance of children (that is, their "right intentions" to enter into Marriage validly); the consent, by which the couple gives themselves to each other in Marriage; the reception of the consent, which includes the statement of reception by the priest and a response by the assembly; the blessing and giving of rings; and the Universal Prayer (Prayer of the Faithful). A rubric indicates that all stand during the Celebration of Matrimony.[72] This is not new to the ritual text, but it is not often common practice. This particular posture of the assembly might engage them more actively in the action of prayer taking place rather than for them to remain seated as spectators.

There is no instruction regarding where this takes place, although the established custom is to have the couple stand in the center of the sanctuary before the altar, accompanied by their witnesses and the bridal party. The priest or deacon should stand in such a way that he can effectively officiate while still allowing the assembly to see and hear what is taking place between the bride and groom. For example, the priest or deacon may stand in front of the altar facing the couple and the congregation. Or he may stand within the congregation facing the couple but off to the side so not to obstruct the assembly's view of the ritual action. The arrangement of the officiant, couple, witnesses, and other members of the bridal party really depends upon the size of the space within the sanctuary and its visibility from the liturgical assembly. This latter arrangement emphasizes the couple as the ministers of the sacrament. The priest or deacon may invite the couple to come forward for the Celebration of Matrimony.[73]

Address to the Couple and Witnesses

The Celebration of Matrimony begins with an address to the couple and to their witnesses. Text is provided in the ritual although the priest or deacon may revise or write their own text using similar words. The text in the rite recognizes that the couple have come into the "house of the Church"—in

---

72 See OCM, 59.

73 The rite also notes, "If two or more Marriages happen to be celebrated at the same time, the Questions before the Consent, the Consent itself, and also the Reception of the Consent must always take place individually for each Marriage; the remaining parts, however, including the Nuptial Blessing, should be spoken once for all in the plural" (OCM, 58).

the presence of "the community"—with the intention to enter into the Sacrament of Matrimony which "strengthens" what God has already "consecrated by Holy Baptism."[74]

Questions before the Consent

Before the couple gives their consent, the priest or deacon must question them about their intentions to marry. A series of three questions are asked concerning their "freedom of choice, fidelity to each other, and the acceptance and upbringing of children."[75] Each responds separately to the questions. The question concerning children may be omitted if, for example, a couple is older or cannot have children.[76]

Forms of the Consent

The consent of the spouses is the essential form of the Celebration of Matrimony. Couples must use the texts that are provided in the rite and not substitute them with "vows" they have written themselves. When giving the proper consent, the couple expresses their promise to each other, and in doing so they enter into a covenant with one another:

When giving consent, the couple joins their right hands.

> I, **N.** take you, **N.** to be my wife/husband.
> I promise to be faithful to you,
> in good times and in bad,
> in sickness and in health,
> to love you and to honor you
> all the days of my life.[77]

In the dioceses of the United States, a second form of consent may be used. The alternate form is understood by some to be "ecumenical" in that it is found in other rituals and is often used even in civil ceremonies, but it is actually based on a text found in the Sarum

---

74 OCM, 59.
75 OCM, 60.
76 See OCM, 60.
77 OCM, 62.

Rite.[78] At the suggestion of the Vatican Congregation for Divine Worship and the Discipline of the Sacraments, an addition has been made to the text (addition in bold) in the new edition:

> I, **N.**, take you, **N.**, for my lawful wife/husband
> to have and to hold from this day forward
> for better, for worse,
> for richer, for poorer,
> in sickness and in health,
> **to love and to cherish**
> until death do us part.[79]

With either form of the consent, the ritual presumes that under normal circumstances the groom and the bride will speak the words of consent themselves. The rubric simply states, 'The bridegroom says/The bride says."[80] There is no mention of how this happens. Customarily the groom and the bride repeat the vows phrase-by-phrase after the priest or deacon. They could, however, be asked to memorize the text of the consent so that they can speak the words intact and without interruption. This also invites the couple to spend significant time reflecting on the promises they will make, and the priest or deacon might suggest that they memorize the words not only for the wedding day but for the whole of their married life. If memorization seems unfeasible, the couple could also read the text of consent from the ritual text (held before them by a server or other assisting minister). The rite also suggests that if "it seems preferable for pastoral reasons, the Priest may obtain the consent of the contracting parties through questioning."[81] Although this is clearly not the preferred practice, the rite does provide the text for the question and answer format.[82] The priest or deacon directs the questions to the couple separately. Their response is "I do."

> **N.**, do you take **N.**, to be your wife/husband?
> Do you promise to be faithful to her/him
> in good times and in bad,
> in sickness and in health,

---

78 The Sarum Rite, or more accurately, the "Sarum Use," is an eleventh century application of the Roman Rite in Anglo-Saxon lands. The *Book of Common Prayer* makes use of many texts that have evolved from the Sarum Use.

79 OCM, 62; emphasis added.

80 OCM, 62.

81 OCM, 63

82 See OCM, 63.

to love her/him and to honor her/him
all the days of your life?[83]

Or:

N., do you take **N.** for your lawful wife/husband,
to have and to hold, from this day forward,
for better, for worse,
for richer, for poorer,
in sickness and in health,
to love and to cherish
until death do you part?[84]

Reception of Consent

Once the spouses have given their consent, the priest "receives"[85] or accepts
their consent. It is important to note that the priest does not "pronounce" or
"declare" the couple to be husband and wife, but announces, rather, that God
has joined them together, for it is the couple who give themselves to each
other in Marriage. As noted earlier, the role of the priest is to "officiate" as
the representative of the Church and the civil jurisdiction. This is further
indicted by the lack of any particular gestures by the priest throughout the
Celebration of Matrimony. There is no blessing or invocation over the couple
(only over the rings). The rite includes an alternate form of the reception of
consent that invokes the Patriarchs of the Old Testament as a reminder that
Marriage is established by God from the beginning.

Option 1

May the Lord in his kindness strengthen the consent
you have declared before the Church,
and graciously bring to fulfillment his blessing within you.
What God joins together, let no one put asunder.[86]

Option 2

May the God of Abraham, the God of Isaac, the God of Jacob,
the God who joined together our first parents in paradise,
strengthen and bless in Christ

---

83 OCM, 63.
84 OCM, 63; emphasis added.
85 See OCM, 64.
86 OCM, 64.

the consent you have declared before the Church,
so that what God joins together, no one may put asunder.[87]

The assembly is then invited to give praise to God in response to the reception of the consent. Whereas the previous *Rite of Marriage* (1969) simply suggested that the assembly give its "assent" by responding, "Amen,"[88] the second edition of the rite is more focused on praising God for what has taken place, and there is flexibility regarding the assembly's response in an acclamation which may be sung. The priest "invites those present to praise God" by saying, "Let us bless the Lord." The assembly responds, "Thanks be to God."[89] "Another acclamation may be sung or said"[90] as well.

How to enact this dialogue will be a particular challenge, since one cannot presume that those gathered as the liturgical assembly will be familiar with the response. Inclusion of the dialogue in a printed worship aid will

The assembly is invited to sing an acclamation of praise after the reception of the consent.

be necessary. The use of "another acclamation" could be an easier alternative. A sung "Amen" (perhaps the same musical setting of the "Amen" used in the Eucharistic Prayer) will be easy, although, "Amen," which means "I believe" or "So be it," does not fully express the sentiment of praising God that is called for. A setting of the "Alleluia," which means "Praise God," is just as easy to engage and is more fitting as an acclamation (except during Lent, of course). Still more appropriate is a psalm refrain that praises God. Several refrains from within *The Order of Celebrating Matrimony* would be appropriate, especially if the same psalm refrain is used as the Responsorial Psalm (this provides consistency and familiarity with the various acclamations of the liturgy). Examples from the rite are found on the next page.

---

87 OCM, 64.

88 See the first edition of the *Rite of Marriage* (1969), 26.

89 OCM, 65.

90 OCM, 65.

- I will bless the Lord at all times.[91]

- Taste and see the goodness of the Lord.[92]

- Let all praise the name of the Lord.[93]

The Blessing and Giving of Rings

The spouses exchange rings as a sign of their commitment. The *praenotanda* notes that "the rings for the spouses should be prepared in the sanctuary."[94] The rings could be placed on a small table near where the vessel with holy water will be placed to accommodate for the blessing. Similar to the explanatory rites in Baptism (the anointing with chrism after Baptism, the presentation of the lighted candle and the white garment), this symbolic gesture sheds more light on the mystery being celebrated. The *Rite of Christian Initiation of Adults* describes the function of the explanatory rites of Baptism in this way: "The baptismal washing is followed by rites that give expression to the effects of the sacrament just received."[95] The rings are blessed by

The giving of rings is a primary sign of unity in the wedding liturgy.

the priest, who may also sprinkle them with holy water.[96] This has been the customary practice, but the earlier edition of the *Rite of Marriage* never mentioned sprinkling the rings with holy water.[97] The "vessel of holy water with an aspergillum"[98] should be prepared in the sanctuary ahead of time.

The dialogue provided by the rite for the couple when exchanging rings is optional. The earlier edition of the rite indicated that the bride and the groom "may say" the formula.[99] The rubric now indicates, "The husband

---

91 Psalm 34 (33):2a; OCM, 168; Lectionary, 803.2.

92 Psalm 34 (33):9a; OCM, 168; Lectionary, 803.2.

93 Psalm 148:13a; OCM, 173; Lectionary, 803.7.

94 OCM, 38. Note that the ring bearer is not part of the Church's official ritual.

95 *Rite of Christian Initiation of Adults* (RCIA), 214.

96 See OCM, 66.

97 Texts are found at OCM, 66 (within Mass). This same text is used for the Celebration of Matrimony without Mass (OCM, 100) and with a Catechumen or Non-Christian (OCM, 131). Alternate texts may be used and are found at OCM, 194 and 195 (chapter IV, part III, Other Prayers for the Blessing of Rings).

98 OCM, 38.

99 See *Rite of Marriage* (1969), 28.

places his wife's ring on her ring finger, saying, as the circumstances so suggest"[100] and vice versa. On the one hand, the symbol could speak for itself without the need for words, but on the other hand, the words, "as a sign of my love and fidelity"[101] make clear the intention of the gesture.

Hymn or Canticle of Praise

After the giving of the rings,[102] the whole assembly ("community") may sing a hymn or canticle of praise.[103] This new addition to the ritual serves as yet another way to engage the liturgical assembly in an act of worship. Selecting a hymn or song that praises God for the particular work of grace in the Sacrament of Matrimony will be essential if this act is to be effective. The ritual is clear that this is not the time for solo music or meditation, nor should the hymn or song merely express sentiments about the couple and their love for one another. One could consider simply repeating the acclamation of praise which was sung after the reception of consent as an abbreviated form of praise in keeping with the spirit of the moment without having to introduce another unfamiliar piece of music.

Universal Prayer (Prayer of the Faithful)

The Celebration of Matrimony concludes with the Universal Prayer, in which the gathered assembly offers prayers for the Church, the world, the oppressed, and the local community (the newly married couple).[104] The rubric indicates that this takes place "in the usual manner."[105] Two examples are provided in chapter III of the ritual text. Both examples include intentions for the couple, for the families and friends gathered, for all married couples and those preparing for Marriage, and for those in need. Many resources available to couples provide other samples which can be used as a guide when couples are invited to prepare their own intentions or to suggest intentions to include.[106] In particular, this is a customary time to remember deceased members of the families of the bride and groom, or intentions that are of particular concern to those gathered and of the local community. Those who are assisting couples in their preparation process might find it beneficial to work together with

---

100 See OCM, 67A.

101 OCM, 67A.

102 If the Blessing and Giving of the *Arras* is done, it takes place at this time (OCM, 67b); see page 63 for pastoral commentary.

103 OCM, 68.

104 Sample texts are provided in the OCM in the appendix, part I.

105 OCM, 69.

106 See the "Resources" section on page 107.

the couples to craft the intentions in order to help them grow in their own ability to pray for particular needs. The petitions may be read by a deacon, a reader, or sung by the cantor. Place the prayer in a binder for both the presider and the reader of the petitions.

The Creed

Following the Universal Prayer the "Creed is said, if required by the rubrics"[107]; for example, if the wedding is taking place on a solemnity or during Sunday Mass. Notice that the Creed *follows* the Universal Prayer rather than taking place *before*. Either the Nicene Creed or Apostles' Creed may be said. Use the Creed that is usually done in your parish community.

Liturgy of the Eucharist

The Liturgy of the Eucharist takes place as usual. *The Order of Celebrating Matrimony* includes the option for the bride and the groom to bring forward the gifts of bread and wine at the Preparation of the Gifts. Of course, family members or friends of the couple may do so instead. Music ministers should advise couples to select musical settings for the acclamations and songs for the reception of Communion that will be familiar to those gathered for the wedding. A hymn or chant may be selected for the Preparation of the Gifts and a congregational song should be selected for the distribution and reception of Communion.[108] The gifts, altar, and cross may be incensed during the Preparation of the Gifts, as well as the couple and the assembly. During the Eucharistic Prayer, the couple, witnesses, and other attendants should assume the same posture of the worshipping assembly.[109] The Prayer over the Offerings is found in both the Ritual Masses for Marriage in the Missal as well is in chapter IV, part IV, in *The Order of Celebrating Matrimony*. The Prefaces are also found in the same section in the Missal and in part V of the ritual book for Marriage.[110] Presiders will need *The Roman Missal* for the Eucharistic Prayer.

---

107 OCM, 69.

108 Although STL indicates that a solo may be sung during the Preparation of the Gifts and after Communion; however, solos should be carefully considered in light of the ritual action taking place and should only occur "provided the music and their manner of singing does not call attention to themselves but rather assists in the contemplation of the sacred mysteries being celebrated" (221). Congregational singing should always be the preference and couples should be encouraged to select music that involves the "full, conscious, and active participation" of the entire assembly (see CSL, 14).

109 See also page 44.

110 See OCM, 199-201.

Eucharistic Prayers I, II, and III should be used with the Ritual Mass (since Eucharistic Prayer IV has a proper Preface). Among the new elements included in the third edition of *The Roman Missal* is the special commemoration of the married couple to be used in Eucharistic Prayers I, II, and III. The previous *Sacramentary* included a special form of the *Hanc igitur* in Eucharistic Prayer I (The Roman Canon), but nothing had been provided for use with Eucharistic Prayers II or III.

In Eucharistic Prayer I

The proper form of the Hanc igitur *(Therefore, Lord, we pray) is said. The words in parentheses may be omitted, if the occasion so suggests.*

Therefore, Lord, we pray:
graciously accept this oblation of our service,
the offering of your servants **N.** and **N.**
and of your whole family,
who entreat your majesty on their behalf;
and as you have brought them to their wedding day,
so (gladden them with your gift of the children they desire and)
bring them in your kindness
to the length of days for which they hope.
(Through Christ our Lord. Amen.)[111]

In Eucharistic Prayer II

After the words and all the clergy, *the following is added:*

Be mindful also, Lord, of **N.** and **N.**,
whom you have brought to their wedding day,
so that by your grace
they may abide in mutual love and in peace.[112]

In Eucharistic Prayer III

After the words whom you have summoned before you, *the following is added:*

Strengthen, we pray, in the grace of Marriage **N.** and **N.**,
whom you have brought happily to their wedding day,
that under your protection
they may always be faithful in their lives
to the covenant they have sealed in your presence.

---

111 OCM, 202.
112 OCM, 203.

In your compassion, O merciful Father,
gather to yourself all your children
scattered throughout the world.[113]

These texts are found in the Ritual Mass propers for Marriage in *The Roman Missal*, as well as in chapter V of *The Order of Celebrating Matrimony*.[114] As a practical note, it might be easier for celebrants, as a means of avoiding an awkward page turn during the Eucharistic Prayer, to reprint these texts on small cards that can be tucked in at the proper page within the Missal.

The Roman Missal and the revised Marriage Rite include special inserts to use at weddings when praying Eucharistic Prayers I, II, and III.

Communion Rite
The Nuptial Blessing

The forms of the Nuptial Blessing have been amended in *The Order of Celebrating Matrimony,* Second Edition, and since they are included as proper texts of the Nuptial Mass, they were included in the third edition of *The Roman Missal*, so they have already been introduced into liturgical use.[115]

The Nuptial Blessing takes place immediately after the Lord's Prayer.[116] The embolism and the *Pax Domini* ("Lord, Jesus Christ, who said to your Apostles . . .") are omitted. The rubric indicates that the priest stands facing the bride and groom.[117] The bride and groom, meanwhile, approach the altar, or they may kneel "at their place."[118] All of this seems to indicate that the priest remains at the altar. If the couple's place is too distant from the altar or outside the sanctuary, it is most effective to invite the couple to come forward and stand in front of the altar for the blessing rather than for the priest

---

113 OCM, 204.

114 See OCM, 202–204.

115 The Nuptial Blessings are also included in the OCM at numbers 74, 207, and 209. The chant settings for the blessings are found in the OCM, chapter IV, part II, Other Prayers of Nuptial Blessings (205–209); see also page 24.

116 Although the Lord's Prayer may be chanted, consider the assembly who will be gathered for the wedding. This prayer is a sign of unity among the baptized. If chanting the text will prohibit their participation, it may be better to recite the prayer. Note also that if the Blessing and Placing of the *Lazo* or the Veil will take place, it is done after the Our Father and before the Nuptial Blessing (see page 65).

117 See OCM, 72.

118 OCM, 73.

to leave the altar since the blessing is connected to the actions at the altar. Joining his hands, the priest invites "those present to pray."[119] After the invitation to prayer, the priest extends both his hands over the couple as he prays the blessing. Notice the invitation to prayer is followed by a period of silence. After the blessing, "The peace of the Lord" is said and the Sign of Peace takes place.[120] It is interesting to note that the rubric indicates that the exchange of the Sign of Peace in this context is not optional.[121]

Each of the forms of the Nuptial Blessing includes a clear invocation of the Holy Spirit, an "epiclesis" over the *couple* not over only the bride. This is why the priest or deacon (at Marriages without Mass) is to extend his hands over the couple:

Option 1

Look now with favor on these your servants,
joined together in Marriage,
who ask to be strengthened by your blessing.
Send down on them the grace of the Holy Spirit
and pour your love into their hearts,
that they may remain faithful in the Marriage covenant.[122]

Option 2

Graciously stretch out your right hand
over these your servants (**N.** and **N.**), we pray,
and pour into their hearts the power of the Holy Spirit.[123]

Option 3

May your abundant blessing, Lord,
come down upon this bride, **N.**,
and upon **N.**, her companion for life,
and may the power of your Holy Spirit
set their hearts aflame from on high,
so that, living out together the gift of Matrimony,
they may (adorn their family with children
and) enrich the Church.[124]

---

119 OCM, 73.

120 See OCM, 75.

121 See also pages 60 and 69 regarding the Sign of Peace.

122 OCM, 74.

123 OCM, 207.

124 OCM, 209. The fourth option for the Nuptial Blessing is for the Celebration of Matrimony between a Catholic and a Catechumen or a Non-Christian (OCM, 138-140) and is addressed on page 61.

The Nuptial Blessing developed during the period of the Roman Sacramentaries, the earliest complete forms of liturgical books in the latter part of the first Christian millennium. The Communion Rite (before the *Pax Domini*) was frequently the context for these blessings. Today the Nuptial Blessing remains as the last vestige of the medieval practice. The only other similar practice is the traditional arrangement of the Blessing of the Oils and the Consecration of the Chrism at the Chrism Mass on Holy Thursday.[125] Today, the Nuptial Blessing functions as a seal on the couple prior to their sharing in Communion together. In some respect, the blessing, not unlike the Sign of Peace, is a fruit or effect of the Real Presence of Christ in the Eucharist. One might also note that the "epiclesis" over the couple, then, follows appropriately after the invocation of the Spirit upon the Eucharistic offering and upon the Church within the Eucharistic Prayer.

While there is historic and theological significance to the placement of the Nuptial Blessing here, it is not without its challenges. For many this is experienced as an anomaly in the liturgy because it is such an unfamiliar structure. A brief explanation to those gathered at the rehearsal might help participants, especially the couple, to experience the richness of the tradition.[126] Perhaps a notation in the printed program or worship aid would also help those gathered at the wedding to understand and appreciate the significance of the ritual.

Receiving Communion

Once the bride and groom have been sealed by the Nuptial Blessing, their first act as a newly married couple is to share together in Holy Communion. The ritual indicates that they, and all gathered, may receive Communion under both kinds,[127] and this is most fitting as the sharing in the one Bread and the one Cup becomes a sign of the union of those who partake in it. Priests and those who assist couples with preparation will need to consider the need for other ministers to assist with the distribution of Communion, either by making use of deacons, acolytes, or extraordinary ministers of Holy Communion from the parish; members of the family who are extraordinary ministers; or by deputizing qualified individuals for the particular occasion.

---

125 During which the Blessing of the Oil of the Sick takes place at the end of the Eucharistic Prayer but before the final doxology. The Oil of Catechumens is blessed and the Sacred Chrism is consecrated after the Prayer after Communion, although it is permitted to conduct all the blessings during the Liturgy of the Word.

126 See also page 83.

127 See OCM, 76.

Some priests even suggest that the bride and groom themselves serve as extraordinary ministers, which may be desirable in circumstances in which the faith and devotion of the couple warrants it, but one should not presume to do this as common practice in all circumstances.

As noted earlier, it is best if congregational singing accompanies the Communion Procession. The Communion Song begins as the priest receives Communion and continues until all have received.[128] If there are large numbers of people receiving Communion it may be necessary to select more than one Communion Song.[129] Accomplished musicians can transition the songs together instrumentally so that the ritual action is unified musically, rather than as songs performed separately. Songs with a refrain will be easier for the assembly to participate.[130] The options for the Communion Antiphon are found in the Missal. Music ministers should note that during Easter Time an Alleluia is added to the antiphon.

> Because the Communion chant expresses the unity of those processing and receiving the Holy Sacrament, communal singing is commendable. The singing of the people should be preeminent.
>
> —*Sing to the Lord: Music in Divine Worship*, 189

Option A

Christ loved the Church and handed himself over for her,
to present her as a holy and spotless bride for himself.

—Cf. Ephesians 5:25, 27

Option B

I give you a new commandment, that you love one another
as I have loved you, says the Lord.

—John 13:34

Option C

I will bless the Lord at all times,
praise of him is always in my mouth.
Taste and see that the Lord is good;
blessed the man who seeks refuge in him.

—Psalm 34 (33):2, 9

---

128 See GIRM, 86; see also footnote 108 on page 51.
129 See STL, 193.
130 See STL, 191 and 192.

As noted earlier, the choice of using other songs should be inspired by the intentions expressed here, keeping in mind the abilities of the particular gathered assembly. Music ministers will recognize these options (especially options B and C) as the source text for many familiar Communion songs ("I Have Loved You," "Taste and See," and so on). A song of thanksgiving may follow the Communion song.[131] The assembly may stand for the song of thanksgiving.[132]

At every celebration of the Eucharist, those who are gathered unite themselves to the one sacrifice of Christ that becomes present at the altar. They do so by offering the gifts of bread and wine which will become the Body and Blood of Christ. At a wedding, the sacrifice the newly married couple offers to each other is also symbolized as they bring forth these gifts. Presiders should be sure to consecrate enough hosts and wine for the entire assembly. This way all can participate in the offering of the Eucharistic sacrifice present at that Mass. The *General Instruction of the Roman Missal* states:

> "It is most desirable that the faithful, just as the Priest himself is bound to do, receive the Lord's Body from hosts consecrated at the same Mass and that, in the cases where this is foreseen, they partake of the chalice, so that even by means of the signs Communion may stand out more clearly as a participation in the sacrifice actually being celebrated."[133]

The *General Instruction of the Roman Missal* presumes that parishes are not distributing Communion during Mass by using the reserved sacraments — it does not provide rubrics or directives for how to do so appropriately. It should not be difficult for sacristans or other pastoral ministers to provide enough hosts and wine to be consecrated at the Nuptial Mass, especially since most couples have an exact count of attendees at their wedding. Doing so ensures that their participation in the life-giving meal and sacrifice of the Eucharist is clear, and it maintains the connection between the reserved Sacrament as fulfilling the need for Viaticum, receiving Communion when one is ill or homebound, and the need for prayer in the presence of the Blessed Sacrament. The reserved Sacrament should not be a source for Communion during the Mass.

---

131 See STL, 196.

132 See STL, 196; see also page 51.

133 GIRM, 85; see also GIRM, 283, RS, 89, *Norms for the Distribution and Reception of Holy Communion under Both Kinds in the Dioceses of the United States of America* (NDRHC), 30.

Prayer after Communion

Although there is no rubric indicating that the Prayer after Communion follows the distribution of Communion, three options are provided in *The Order of Celebrating Matrimony* in chapter IV, part VIII, "Prayers after Communion":[134] Presiders should allow for a moment of silence to follow the invitation to pray ("Let us pray").

The Conclusion of the Celebration

Solemn Blessing and Dismissal

Following the Prayer after Communion, the ritual provides several forms of the Solemn Blessing. The Solemn Blessing is not optional.[135] The blessing itself is imparted on the *couple*, and the priest is to extend his hands over them. Following the threefold blessing, the final blessing is given over *everyone*. In order to indicate the difference between the two blessings, the final blessing is unique for this particular ritual text:

> And may almighty God bless all of you, *who are gathered here*,
> the Father, and the Son, ✚ and the Holy Spirit.
> R. Amen.[136]

The dismissal, "Go in peace" (or other forms), is not provided in the ritual. It can be presumed that texts from the Order of Mass are included unless they are explicitly omitted, as in the case of several elements indicated earlier: the Penitential Act and the embolism after the Lord's Prayer. "Go in peace, glorifying the Lord by your life" appropriately points to the vocational responsibilities of the newly married couple.

The rite also does not mention a procession or any kind of singing at this point, although these may certainly occur.[137] By custom, however, a procession led by the bride and groom normally takes place. It is appropriate for all to make a sign of reverence to the altar (or to the tabernacle if present) upon leaving the sanctuary. The priest and other ministers would make the

---

134 See OCM, 210-212. They are also found in the Ritual Masses V., For the Celebration of Marriage.

135 See OCM, 77.

136 OCM, 77; emphasis added.

137 A closing song is not part of the Eucharistic liturgy; however, it has become a custom in the United States. Although it is more common for instrumental music to accompany the closing procession, a hymn or song expressing joy and praise for what has taken place in the Nuptial Mass may also be chosen. This might be requested by a couple, for example, who is actively involved in music ministry.

customary sign of reverence and depart the sanctuary as well. If servers bearing the cross and candles led the Entrance Procession, then they could also lead the bride and groom during the recession at this time, in which case the priest and the other ministers should also follow behind the bridal party.

The only final indication in the text is the instruction regarding the signing of the Marriage record, which may be done in the presence of the people or in private, but it is never to take place on the altar.

Celebrating Matrimony without Mass

The choice of the form of the Celebration of Matrimony was addressed earlier in this chapter.[138] Here all that remains is to discuss the structure of the ritual. All of the essential elements of the Celebration of Matrimony within Mass are the same, along with the possible inclusion of the optional cultural rituals.[139] There is the possibility of distributing Communion, although this would seemingly only occur in cases in which the Nuptial Mass would otherwise be celebrated but no priest is available to do so. In this case the deacon is acting in the absence of a priest.[140]

If Mass is not celebrated, the Celebration of Matrimony still takes place after the homily.

The Introductory Rites take place in the same way, with the exception of the Gloria, which is only sung or said in the celebration of Mass. Immediately after the Sign of the Cross and greeting (alternate forms may be used from the Missal), the priest or deacon addresses the couple and the gathered assembly. Then, with hands extended, he prays one of the Collects.

The Liturgy of the Word takes place in the usual manner, with the same provision that one of the readings chosen must explicitly speak of Marriage.

The Celebration of Matrimony takes place after the homily in the same way as outlined above. The Universal Prayer (Prayer of the Faithful) takes

138 See page 29.
139 See page 63.
140 See page 23.

place as well, although its concluding prayer is omitted and all are invited to pray the Lord's Prayer.[141] The Nuptial Blessing follows, and the final blessing of all the people takes place.

If Communion is to be distributed, such as in the case of a Marriage between two Catholics officiated by a deacon when a priest is not available, then the order is slightly altered: the concluding prayer of the Universal Prayer is offered,[142] followed by the Nuptial Blessing. Then the deacon goes to the place of reservation of the Blessed Sacrament and brings the ciborium to the altar. All pray the Lord's Prayer, and then the deacon may invite the people to exchange a Sign of Peace. The invitation to and distribution of Communion follows. An appropriate antiphon or song is sung during the distribution of Communion.[143] Use the Prayer after Communion that is found in the ritual text for this form of the celebration. The rubric specifically notes "the minister says this prayer":[144]

During this form of the rite, the priest or deacon may be vested in an alb and stole.

> Having been made partakers at your table,
> we pray, O Lord,
> that those who are united by the Sacrament of Marriage
> may always hold fast to you
> and proclaim your name to the world.
> Through Christ our Lord.[145]

Some may wonder why this prayer must be said instead of the other two options found in the rite and the Missal.[146] These prayers specifically mention the "sacrifice" which implies that Mass took place, whereas the option noted above refers to those who have "been made partakers at your

---

141 The Blessing and Giving of the *Arras* may take place at this time; see page 64.

142 The Blessing and Placing of the *Lazo* or the Veil may take place at this time; see page 65.

143 See GIRM, 87.

144 OCM, 115.

145 This prayer is also found at OCM, 211, and in the Ritual Masses for Marriage, option B. This prayer may be used in place of the other options if Mass is celebrated.

146 See OCM, 210 and 212.

table." The action of the Eucharistic sacrifice offered at the Mass is not implied in this prayer.

The conclusion of the celebration varies and will depend upon whether or not Communion is distributed. If Communion is not distributed, the "minister immediately blesses the people"[147] after the Nuptial Blessing. There is no Solemn Blessing. Although not mentioned in the rite, the dismissal takes place (using any of the three forms provided in the Order of Mass). This form of the rite includes the option for a concluding song or chant: "It is a praiseworthy practice to end the celebration with a suitable chant,"[148] but no mention is made of suggested texts to be used. This is separate and distinct from the hymn or canticle of praise that may follow the blessing and giving of rings, although they appear to have a similar function, and one might consider making use of one or the other, but not both.[149]

If Communion is distributed, following the Prayer after Communion the minister may offer one of the Solemn Blessings over the couple, and then the blessing of the people. The dismissal follows. The rite does not mention a concluding song or chant.

Celebrating Matrimony between a Catholic and a Catechumen or a Non-Christian

The structure of the ritual for the Celebration of Matrimony between a Catholic and a Catechumen or a Non-Christian generally follows the structure of Matrimony without Mass while making use of several texts that are specific to this unique pastoral situation. This celebration can take place either in a church or "another suitable place,"[150] so the rubric regarding the arrangement of the place is left somewhat vague.

The ritual begins with the Rite of Reception: the priest or deacon greets the couple at the entrance, and then the procession of the ministers, the couple, and the witnesses takes place as they "go to the seats prepared for each one."[151] No specific norms are given. There is no Sign of the Cross, but the priest or

---

147 OCM, 106.

148 OCM, 107.

149 On page 50, it was suggested in place of the hymn or canticle to sing the same acclamation that was sung following the Reception of the Consent. If this is done, it may be appropriate to sing a closing song.

150 OCM, 118; see also canon 112.7

151 OCM, 119.

deacon begins by addressing the people, and a sample address is provided.[152] Note the distinction about how "believers" look to God:

> **N.** and **N.**, the Church shares your joy
> and warmly welcomes you,
> together with your families and friends,
> as today you establish between yourselves
> a lifelong partnership.
> For believers God is the source of love and fidelity,
> because God is love.[153]

The Liturgy of the Word takes place in the usual manner, except that "there may be one or two readings."[154] Still, the provision is in place that one reading must explicitly speak of Marriage.[155]

The Celebration of Matrimony follows the same structure, although the introductory address is modified to omit mention of the celebration of a sacrament. The Universal Prayer follows after the blessing and giving of rings.[156]

New to this edition of the ritual is the arrangement of the Lord's Prayer (this was optional in the previous edition), which now follows the invocations of the Universal Prayer (that is, the concluding prayer of the Universal Prayer is omitted). The rite notes that it is the Christians who pray the Lord's Prayer.[157] Since this prayer is specific to the baptized, pastoral ministers may wonder how to handle this appropriately so that the unbaptized are not made to feel unwelcome. The rite provides a special invitation to the Lord's Prayer which addresses this concern in a pastoral manner:

> God the Father wills that his children be of one heart in charity;
> let those who are Christian call upon him
> in the prayer of God's family,
> which our Lord Jesus Christ has taught us:[158]

---

152 See OCM, 120.
153 OCM, 120.
154 OCM, 122.
155 See also page 38.
156 The Blessing and Giving of the *Arras* may take place after the Blessing and Giving of Rings; the Blessing and Placing of the *Lazo* or the Veil may take place after the Our Father; see also page 63.
157 See OCM, 136.
158 OCM, 136.

A special form of the Nuptial Blessing is also provided, as is a provision that the Nuptial Blessing can be omitted altogether,[159] in which case another prayer is provided (adapted from *The Roman Missal*, Nuptial Mass, C):

> Be attentive to our prayers, O Lord,
> and in your kindness uphold
> what you have established for the increase of the human race,
> so that the union you have created
> may be kept safe by your assistance.
> Through Christ our Lord.
> **R.** Amen.[160]

Then the priest or deacon blesses all gathered in the usual way. There is no option provided for a Solemn Blessing. Again, there is mention of the use of a "suitable chant" to conclude the celebration.[161]

Cultural Adaptations in *The Order of Celebrating Matrimony*

Around the world the Celebration of Matrimony is influenced by cultural traditions, customs, and adaptations, and the authority to suggest such adaptations belongs to the territorial Conference of Bishops. Included in *The Order of Celebrating Matrimony* are two optional customs that may be added to the ritual. These customs were included in the Spanish edition of the ritual (published in the dioceses of the United States in 2010) and were translated for use in the English second edition of the rite. The blessing and exchange of coins (*arras*) and the blessing and placing of the cords or garland (*lazo*) or veil are frequently incorporated into the Celebration of Matrimony in Hispanic communities and in some Asian communities as well. The intention for their inclusion was originally for use in multilingual celebrations or with families from those cultures where these particular customs are commonplace. The use of these rituals goes back to some of the earliest Christian Marriage rituals, so wider use of these gestures (beyond particular ethnic groups or cultures) could be suggested by their arrangement in the text.

---

159 See OCM, 138.
160 OCM, 140.
161 OCM, 143.

The *Arras* or Coins

The blessing and exchange of coins in medieval rites represented the dowry that would have been given to the groom.[162] Today the coins represent the fidelity of the couple and the commitment of the groom to support the bride. The exchange of coins (*arras*) may take place immediately after the blessing and giving of rings regardless if the liturgy is within or without Mass or with a catechumen or non-Christian.

The rubrics in *The Order of Celebrating Matrimony* are rather vague, which suggests room for cultural adaptation. There is neither any mention of where the coins are placed nor whether they are presented by selected individuals. In Hispanic cultures, there are usually twelve or thirteen copper, gold, or silver coins that are placed in a small box. The number thirteen, a baker's dozen, represents each of the twelve months of the year plus an additional gift to share with the poor, signifying the welfare and prosperity of the new family and its care for and charity given toward those who are less fortunate. The number thirteen is also thought to bring good luck in Hispanic cultures, (although of course this is superstition and has no bearing on the sacramental rite itself).

The custom is usually to have the bride and groom select a married couple to present the box with the coins. This couple is known as the *padrinos* and are usually godparents or a sponsor couple. This couple may be from the bride or groom's side of the family. The couple will need to decide together whom they would like to present the coins:

> "*Padrinos* hold a very special place in Hispanic cultures since they represent God's graces and blessing. In fact, they become an integral part of the family and hold a place of respect in it. As is true of any parent, this entails certain obligations toward the *ahijado*, the godchild. To be asked to be a godparent is considered a great honor even when it implies helping with the expenses of the wedding."[163]

---

162 "The word *arras* comes from the Greek word *arrabon*, which means 'pledge,' and originally referred to the giving of 'earnest money,' or dowry. In parts of the Latin West, the actual exchange of vows borrowed this term and was called the *ordo arrarum*, or 'the rite of pledges,' and coins sealed the pledge." As noted in Mark R. Francis and Arturo J. Pérez-Rodríguez, *Primero Dios: Hispanic Liturgical Resource* (Chicago, Illinois: Liturgy Training Publications, 1997), p. 100.

163 Rev. Raúl Gomez, SDS, Rev. Heliodoro Lucatero, and Sylvia Sánchez, members of the Instituto Nacional Hispano de Liturgia [National Hispanic Institute of Liturgy], *Gift and Promise: Customs and Traditions in Hispanic Rites of Marriage*, 2nd ed. (Portland, Oregon: Oregon Catholic Press, 1997, 2005), p. 9.

When it is time for the *arras* to be exchanged, the priest calls the couple forward who then present him with the box of coins to be blessed. The *padrinos* may stand to the side during the blessing. The priest says: "Bless, ✝ O Lord, these *arras* / that **N.** and **N.** will give to each other / and pour over them the abundance of your good gifts."[164] After the priest has blessed the coins, he pours them into the cupped hands of the groom who then hands the coins to his bride while saying, "**N.**, receive these *arras* as a pledge of God's blessing / and a sign of the good gifts we will share."[165] The bride, in turn, presents the same coins to her spouse, while saying the same words. Since the ritual book provides the official text for this cultural adaptation, it is appropriate to follow the same model used for the consent, whereby the couple memorizes the text or repeats the text phrase-by-phrase after the priest or deacon.

After the couple has exchanged the coins, the groom may place the coins back in the box which is then returned to the *padrinos*. The *padrinos* may be seated at this time.[166] The rite does not mention the use of holy water for the blessing. Since it does so for the blessing of the rings, this is most likely an intentional omission in order to allow the blessing of the rings to stand as the primary symbol of unity within the Celebration of Matrimony.[167]

The *Lazo* or Veil

The image of the *lazo* (wedding garland) or veil over the couple is a sign of blessing as well as of joining or binding. The *lazo* or the veil, which are two separate customs, are often passed down from generation to generation in

The blessing and imposition of the *lazo* takes place before the Nuptial Blessing.

---

164 67b, 101b, and 133.

165 OCM, 67b, 101b, and 133.

166 Parish staffs should be aware that some couples may request that the *padrinos* accompany them during the Entrance Procession and be seated with the other witnesses of the wedding. In Hispanic culture, the *padrinos* often serve as the official witnesses whereas in the United States, the best man and maid or matron of honor assume this role.

167 In some Asian cultures, the ring bearer may be selected to bring the coins forward in a drawstring bag rather than a box. The ring bearer is usually given the coins from a male relative of the groom. Any number of coins may be used in Asian cultures rather than twelve or thirteen often used in Hispanic cultures.

families, or they are presented as gifts by members of the family as an expression of their support.

The rite states:

> "According to local customs, the rite of blessing and imposition of the *lazo* (wedding garland) or of the veil may take place before the Nuptial Blessing. The spouses remain kneeling in their place. If the *lazo* has not been placed earlier, and it is now convenient to do so, it may be placed at this time, or else, a veil is placed over the head of the wife and the shoulders of the husband, thus symbolizing the bond that unites them."[168]

After the blessing, "the *lazo* (or the veil) is held by two family members or friends and is placed over the shoulders of the newly married couple."[169]

The rite suggests that either the *lazo* or the veil take place—not both; although, in some cultures, such as in the Philippines, the two are combined. In North American culture, it is more common for the bride to enter the church already veiled. Therefore, the edge of the bride's veil may be placed on (or pinned to) the groom's shoulder. However, in some cultures, an additional veil may be used. The *lazo* may be made from gold, silver, pearls, glass beads, rose blossoms, or a satin rope. It is often formed as a double Rosary with beads and a crucifix. The veil may be a white shawl, mantilla, or made from tulle or lace. The veil represents chastity.

The rite notes that two family members or friends hold the *lazo* or veil while the blessing takes place. Typically, a married couple is chosen to place the *lazo* (cord) or veil (in Hispanic cultures this is the *padrinos*). Regardless as to what form of the Marriage Rite is being used, the presider invites those who will present the *lazo* or veil to come forward after the Lord's Prayer (omitting "Deliver us Lord"). The chosen friends or family members will hold the *lazo* or veil during the blessing and then place the lazo or veil "over the shoulders of the newly married couple." If the veil is already in place, the family members or friends may hold the edge of the veil. If the *lazo* is in the form of a double Rosary, a loop of the cord is placed over each of the newly married couple's shoulders. The crucifix hangs between them. The bride and groom are kneeling while the *lazo* or veil is blessed and placed upon them. If kneelers are not used, a special pillow is placed before the couple to kneel during the blessing and imposition of the *lazo* or veil. Although the rite notes

---

168 OCM, 71b, 103b, and 137.
169 OCM, 71b, 103b, and 137.

that the couple may also stand during the Nuptial Blessing, since they will be kneeling during the blessing and placing of the *lazo* or veil it makes sense for them to remain kneeling during the Nuptial Blessing. After the Nuptial Blessing, the friends or family members remove the *lazo* or veil from the bride and groom and return to their seats.

Adaptations Not in the Rite

In addition to the adaptations approved for inclusion in *The Order of Celebrating Matrimony,* numerous other cultural rituals and contemporary customs are often proposed by couples or suggested as practices particular to individual parish communities or families. Some have dubious origins or questionable meaning, while others may appear harmless or not worth fighting for.

Unity Candle

Although it has become common practice, the unity candle is not part of the Catholic liturgy and its use often overshadows the more important signs of unity that are already within the Celebration of Matrimony. There are many who are quick to point to the Catholic Church as the originator of the "unity candle ceremony" at weddings. It is more likely that the custom had secular origins that caught on as a trend. The unity candle is often a large and elaborately decorated candle flanked by two smaller candles. The couple together lights the unity candle from the two smaller candles as a sign of their union in Marriage. Often the smaller candles are lit by members of the bride's and groom's families. Its exact origin is unclear, although the use of candles in Catholic worship would certainly lead some to presume that the Church had something to do with this rather recent custom. Some have even tried to link the image of the baptismal candle to the unity candle. The symbolism of "two becoming one" in the joining of the light of two candles is not contradictory to what Christians believe about the reality of Marriage; the primary sign of the joining of two as one is the bride and groom themselves and the promises they make in their consent. In Catholic worship, however, candles are seen primarily as a sign of the Light of Christ (particularly linked to the Paschal candle), rather than as a sign of individual persons.

Some parishes and even dioceses have policies restricting or even prohibiting the use of the unity candle in the Celebration of Marriage. Since the unity candle is not part of the Catholic ritual, it is best not to provide its use as an option. However, if it is requested by the couple it is good pastoral practice to suggest that the couple conduct the unity candle ceremony at the wedding reception, perhaps as the couple is first introduced or as they take their place at their table, with the unity candle serving as the centerpiece. Doing so both respects the desires of the couple and the symbolism of the liturgy. Discussing these options with couples becomes a good opportunity to highlight that the spouses themselves and the vows they make, the exchange of rings, and the celebration of the Eucharist are the primary signs of unity in the liturgy. There really is no need to add superfluous symbolism or other elements to the liturgy.

Dedication of Flowers to the Blessed Virgin Mary

Some couples desire to include the custom of taking a bouquet of flowers to the altar or shrine of the Blessed Virgin Mary as an act of devotion, seeking Mary's intercession and prayers for them as they enter into Marriage. This custom is also not part of *The Order of Celebrating Matrimony* and so it would be prudent to ask couples about their particular devotion to Mary if they ask about this ritual, which would be less meaningful when offered by someone with no understanding of the ritual or the devotion from which it flows. Since devotions are of a more personal nature rather than part of communal, liturgical prayer, an alternative, and perhaps, more appropriate form of this gesture might be to offer it as part of a moment of prayer at the wedding rehearsal as the couple seeks the intercession of Mary on the night before their wedding. If parishes and couples do decide to incorporate this devotion into the Nuptial Mass, do so after the Prayer after Communion (so as not to disrupt the integrity and flow of the Communion Rite). Normally, no spoken words accompany the ritual. Instead, a Marian hymn or song, such as the "Ave Maria," may be sung. It is important to note that this ritual should include both the bride and the groom rather than the bride alone or the bride with her bridesmaids or mother. In this way, they enjoy an act of devotion and prayer together as a newly married couple.

Other Customs and Rituals

A variety of other ritual gestures and symbolic elements that are not part of the official rite have found their way into the Marriage liturgy. "Customs" always begin at the grassroots level, and some manage to be passed on from one generation to the next. Some, such as the exchange of coins or the presentation of the *lazo* (cord) or the veil have historical roots and are cherished in certain cultures, while others may appear as novelty and arise out of an attempt by a couple to be unique or to emulate what was done at some other wedding, on television, or online. Among these "customs" are the presentation of flowers to parents of the bride and groom (or to mothers) at the time of the exchange of peace, the inclusion of "sponsor couples" as part of the bridal party (common at weddings of Filipino couples), the blessing and presentation of various devotional articles such as a cross/crucifix, and the custom of "jumping the broom" (occasionally seen at weddings of African American couples).

Couples often feel passionate about a particular ritual or gesture, and if such a ritual has been practiced within a family at many weddings, there may be great pressure to include it in the Marriage liturgy. While respecting the couple's desires and their families' expectations, it is also important to help the couple to understand the real meaning of the particular rituals and how they may or may not harmonize or compete with the nature and purpose of Catholic Marriage rites. Gestures such as the presentation of flowers to parents of the bride and groom at the Sign of Peace might appear as a sign of respect, honor, and love, but mixing such a gesture with the fraternal sharing of the Peace of Christ during the Communion Rite might not be in the best service of the liturgy. At the same time, however, prohibiting such a gesture could complicate the process of preparation with the couple. Maintaining balance between the service of the liturgy and pastoral care for the couple is essential.[170]

Preparation with Couples

Preparing for Marriage entails much more than the liturgical celebration. Sometimes pastoral ministers experience frustration as they notice that couples are more interested in things such as cakes, centerpieces, or menus. Pastoral ministers might identify these things as trivial, or, at least, less important than the celebration of the

I invite all Christians, everywhere, at this very moment, to a renewed personal encounter with Jesus Christ, or at least an openness to letting him encounter them; I ask all of you to do this unfailingly each day. No one should think that this invitation is not meant for him or her, since "no one is excluded from the joy brought by the Lord."

—*Evangelii gaudium*, 3

170 See page 97 for more guidance about this issue.

sacrament, and they are left with one of two responses: either accept the limitations and take a minimalist approach, often resulting in frustration that the situation is not better; or see the situation as an opportunity to invite the couple to a deeper experience of a life-giving encounter, which might take more effort but can have lasting effects.

Many couples who approach the Church regarding Marriage do so in good faith in order to seek the grace of the sacrament. Some, however, do so based on family expectations, pressure from parents or grandparents, or simply because it is the acceptable practice. As pastoral ministers we are called to welcome all and to assist them. Our role is to facilitate their encounter with Jesus Christ in the sacrament. We need to appreciate that some couples can say, "We would like to see Jesus," but others approach the Church because someone else—a relative or friend—said to them, "Come and see." For all of these situations the Church has an obligation to lead engaged couples to Christ so that they may see that he is "the way and the truth and the life."[171]

Pastoral ministers should help couples prepare the liturgical celebration.

The Church invites pastors and all who work with engaged couples to prepare the liturgical celebration together with the couple. The process of preparation itself is a time of formation, and the exercise of making decisions about the Celebration of Matrimony is an opportunity to pray, to reflect on the Scriptures, and to prepare one's heart for the very celebration that is being prepared. *The Order of Celebrating Matrimony* demands that the couple participate in the process of preparation: "The celebration itself of the Sacrament must be diligently prepared, as far as possible, with the engaged couple."[172]

The Order of Celebrating Matrimony suggests that the following ought to be prepared or chosen with the couple:

- the readings from Sacred Scripture
- the form for expressing consent

---

171 John 14:6.
172 OCM, 29.

- the formularies for the blessing of rings and the Nuptial Blessing
- the intentions of the Universal Prayer (Prayer of the Faithful)
- the chants and other musical words
- appropriate use of options provided in the rite, as well as local customs[173]

Why does the rite suggest this, and why is it important? On a practical level, the couple's participation and input assures that the liturgy will reflect their own faith, and it saves both the priest or deacon and the pastoral musician from handling some of the details of the liturgical preparations. More importantly, the couple is able to enter more fully into the mystery being celebrated as they explore the texts and pray over them in order to make decisions. In short, the couple's participation in preparing the rites is part of their "full, conscious, and active participation"[174] in the rites themselves.

> The Church desires that a person's wedding day be filled with joy and grace. When preparing the Liturgy, pastors should address any concerns with the couple with due pastoral sensitivity and sound judgment.
>
> —*Sing to the Lord: Music in Divine Worship*, 217

What does this process look like? Numerous resources are available to assist couples in preparing their part of the wedding liturgy but it is naive to presume that a workbook is all that is necessary. In order to prepare effectively, the engaged couple needs to have an understanding of the nature and purpose of the Sacred Liturgy and a shared vision of what is taking place in the liturgical action. Part of the catechetical process during Marriage preparation necessarily involves some discussion and reflection on the theology of the Sacrament of Matrimony, but it must also include how celebration of the ritual "works," in other words, how the liturgy functions, what the essential components are, and how each of those components contributes to the celebration of the sacrament.

This discussion could take place with the priest, deacon, or with the pastoral musician, or it could take place as part of a Marriage preparation formation session at the parish.[175] A comprehensive preparation worksheet provided by the parish should integrate all the elements of preparation that

---

173 See OCM, 29 and 30.
174 CSL, 14.
175 See page 79 for more guidance about Marriage preparation workshops.

the couple will undertake: the choice of texts, the choice of music, the designation of persons to fill the various roles and ministries, the makeup and order of the Entrance Procession, and so forth.[176]

The actual choices of texts, particularly the Scripture readings, should not be completed at one sitting. It might be suggested to the couple that they

Marriage preparation should help couples learn how to pray together.

take time over the course of several weeks to read prayerfully the various suggested passages (perhaps one reading each day) and then allow some time for reflection, prayer, and discussion together. Each reading, whether it is chosen or not, has something to say to the couple about Marriage. This process will help them learn how to pray together, and could even open up for them new forms of prayer. Consider asking the couple to write a reflection based on the readings they have chosen.

In asking the couple to select the form of the consent, they could be encouraged to spend time reflecting on the meaning and significance of the words they will speak to each other. This will also help them to commit the words to memory for the celebration and for their married life. They should be encouraged to pray over the texts of the Nuptial Blessing as well, in order that their longing for God's grace in the sacrament might focus on what is promised in the blessing.

Hopefully the couple's participation in the preparation process will help them grow in their understanding of the nature and structure of the liturgy so that they will experience it more fully.

Developing a Ministry of Hospitality

Some aspects of parish ministry are very attuned to the need for hospitality, welcome, and a sense of pastoral charity toward those being served or cared for. Caring for those who grieve and mourn at the time of a funeral, welcoming those who are inquiring about the Catholic faith in the Rite of Christian Initiation of Adults, and showing hospitality to newcomers to the parish are but a few examples of situations in which there is normally great

---

176 See page 33 for examples.

effort given to receiving and welcoming others with great care and concern. Procedures and policies for ministering to couples preparing for Marriage is often a different matter, but the aim of ministry to engaged couples is no different than other forms of pastoral ministry: to welcome the person in a spirit of Christian hospitality in order to facilitate a lived encounter with Jesus Christ. Parish staffs and all who work with engaged couples must see this work as ministry and pastoral care rather than merely as a series of business transactions, hurdles to clear, checklists, or requirements to complete.

> The Church must be a place of mercy freely given, where everyone can feel welcomed, loved, forgiven and encouraged to live the good life of the Gospel.
>
> —*Evangelii gaudium*, 114

The process of a warm welcome begins even before a couple calls to inquire about having a wedding. Information provided in the bulletin or on the parish website regarding weddings will set the tone for a couple's experience with the Church. The basic information provided should be inviting and encouraging. Sparing some of the details about policies, limitations in scheduling, fees, or other requirements may help to make a couple feel at ease. Unfortunately many couples see a "church wedding" as only one of several options, so the parish should present an encouraging message that also stresses the importance of the *Sacrament* of Matrimony. This should be seen as an opportunity for evangelization and invitation. There will be plenty of opportunities to outline all the necessary details in one-on-one meetings, an informational brochure, and in group presentations.

The Christ-like presence and demeanor of all parish staff members from the secretary to the pastor is important when ministering to couples.

The initial inquiry by a couple should be treated with sensitivity and care. The first e-mail inquiry or phone call is also a pivotal moment in the process of welcoming and celebrating with a couple. Whoever responds to the inquiry or answers the phone call—whether it is the parish secretary, business manager, liturgist, or pastor— must remember that their presence and demeanor is part of the process of a sacramental encounter, and every conversation and pastoral gesture has the power to help prepare the hearts of the couple for that encounter, just as every conversation and gesture also has the power to build walls and harden hearts.

Priests, deacons, pastoral musicians, and other pastoral ministers know well that not every couple who approaches the parish in preparation for the celebration of their wedding does so with a full understanding of the nature of the sacrament or an appreciation of the Sacred Liturgy, its structures, its values, and, yes, even its rules. There will undoubtedly be moments when the couple's expectations or wishes—or even their predetermined plans—do not coincide or harmonize with the rubrics of the liturgical rites, parish policies and procedures, or the expectations of individual priests, deacons, or musicians. Dealing with disagreements with respect and care for the couple begins with recognizing that they are not at fault for their lack of understanding. Perhaps they have never attended a Catholic wedding themselves, or one of the parties is not Catholic. Perhaps their catechetical formation was incomplete. Whatever the case, see every question or disagreement as a moment for catechesis.

Those who work with engaged couples often have to say no to ideas and suggestions that are not in keeping with the nature of the Sacred Liturgy.

Couples deserve to be treated with care and respect in the name of the Lord.

This can often lead to tense situations, and sometimes compromise is necessary. While the priest or deacon or the pastoral musician might not care for certain choices made by couples, these choices are acceptable choices even if they aren't the ones that "we" would choose. Finding common ground in cases of disagreement can help smooth tension. Pastoral ministers might consider what elements are worth fighting for and which are not. In addition, an explanation about why the Church has certain expectations for the way liturgy is celebrated can also help a couple to appreciate what is important.

Parishes have a variety of polices when it comes to who can have their wedding at the parish. Some parishes restrict access to parishioners only, often because of the size of the parish and the demands of the schedule in the church.[177] Other parishes may welcome those who are not parishioners to celebrate a wedding but may charge a "non-parishioner" rate as a fee (it is important to remember that the Church does not "charge" for the celebration of the sacrament itself, but that such a fee is to defray expenses related to staffing and utilities). Whether the couple inquiring about a wedding are parishioners or not, they still deserve to be treated with care and respect in the name of the Lord.

The Role of the Parish

Except in the rare instances of a Marriage taking place at regularly scheduled Sunday Mass, the parish community may at first glance appear rather absent from the celebration of Marriage of any given couple. Still, the parish community is present and is a valuable part of the process of preparing for and celebrating the sacrament. The prayerful support of the community is—or can be—evident in many ways, and there are ways in which members of the parish community should be involved with the couple during their preparation for Marriage.

> Other laypersons, however, can play a part in various ways both in the spiritual preparation of the engaged couple and in the celebration of the rite itself. Moreover, the entire Christian community should cooperate to bear witness to the faith and to be a sign to the world of Christ's love.
>
> —*The Order of Celebrating Matrimony,* 26

The process of sacramental formation for Marriage, often referred to as "Pre-Cana," typically involves not only the priest or deacon who will officiate but also one or more married couples who, not only by their example but by the instruction they offer, guide an engaged couple and prepare them for the celebration of the sacrament and for living a healthy and holy married life. Parishioners could be invited to offer hospitality and welcome to engaged couples attending group sessions, offer reflections

Parish liturgical ministers may be scheduled to serve at weddings.

---

177 It is important to note that anyone who lives in the defined territory (within the boundaries) is considered a parishioner whether they have ever attended the church or completed a registration form. See the *Code of Canon Law,* canons 515–519.

or presentations during Marriage preparation programs, or be assigned as "mentors" or sponsor couples to individual engaged couples. In some dioceses the "sponsor couple" often serves as the primary agent of formation in a couple-to-couple format.

It is appropriate to commend engaged couples to the prayers of the parish community. Those who prepare the intentions of the Universal Prayer (Prayer of the Faithful) should occasionally include intentions for those preparing for Marriage. The Banns of Marriage serves as an announcement to the parish community of the upcoming Marriages of members of the parish. Historically, announcing the upcoming Marriages provided a way to investigate the ability for someone to enter into the sacrament. Members of the community could step forward to offer concerns, such as if the person in question was already married. Today, the process of Marriage preparation fulfills the same function. Use of the Order of Blessing an Engaged Couple in a public setting will draw attention to those preparing for Marriage and invite the parish's prayerful support for them.[178]

At the time of the celebration of the wedding, parishioners can be invited to serve in a variety of functions from hospitality to particular liturgical functions. One might consider assigning parishioners to serve as greeters for both the rehearsal and the wedding. They can offer assistance by giving directions within the parish buildings, answering questions as people arrive, wel-

Couples may be encouraged to greet their guests as they arrive and distribute worship aids for their ceremony.

coming guests, and assisting the priest or deacon in other ways. Liturgical ministries such as sacristans, servers, and, in some cases, extraordinary ministers of Holy Communion could be carried out by parishioners so that those ministries are fulfilled in an efficient and dignified way. Even when friends or family members of the bride and groom fulfill those roles, a liturgical coordinator from the parish community should be present to assist in training and preparing them or even to guide them during the liturgical celebration itself. While many parishes customarily ask for a stipend for sacristans or servers who assist at weddings, over time many

---

178 See page 77 for more information regarding the Order of Blessing an Engaged Couple.

GUIDE FOR CELEBRATING® MATRIMONY

services such as hospitality or assistance with training ministers can be seen as a natural part of parish ministry that does not demand a stipend or fee. One might even consider including wedding ministry assignments on regular schedules of liturgical ministers. Music ministry is a different case since the pastoral musician's salary usually presumes that separate fees will be earned for weddings and funerals.

The presence and support of the parish community is symbolic, but there are important roles and tasks to be carried out that have both symbolic meaning and practical function, and these should not be overlooked.

Blessing Engaged Couples

The Order of Celebrating Matrimony provides a ritual for the blessing of an engaged couple, which can be used in a variety of circumstances and can serve as a great gesture of hospitality and support for a couple who approaches the parish seeking to celebrate their Marriage. This ritual is a

> May the God of love and peace dwell within you,
> direct your steps,
> and strengthen your hearts in his love.
>
> —"The Order of Blessing an Engaged Couple,"
> *The Order of Celebrating Matrimony*, 235

revised translation of the Order of Blessing an Engaged Couple found in the *Book of Blessings*, and it now supersedes the text found there.[179] The rite is limited to use outside Mass, presumably so that it cannot be confused with the Celebration of Matrimony itself.

Unfortunately, the most public forum in which to offer the blessing, the Sunday Eucharist, is not an option. Normally the blessing is offered soon after a couple is engaged (and the blessing can even be offered, using the proper form, by laypersons, especially by the parents of the couple[180]). There are, however, many creative ways to make use of this ritual which invokes God's blessing upon a couple, or a group of couples, during their Marriage preparation.[181]

To use the blessing as a way to welcome a couple as they begin their preparation, the priest or deacon who meets with the couple could begin their first meeting together with prayer and the offering of the blessing. This could take place in the church, with the priest or deacon offering to escort the couple

179 See *Book of Blessings*, chapter I, part VI.
180 See OCM, 219 and 220.
181 See OCM, 221.

to the sanctuary, where they will eventually stand before the altar on their wedding day, to offer the blessing before proceeding with other matters. This sets a tone for prayer, putting this act of worship and pastoral care before any business of paperwork, discussion of policies, or outline of requirements.

Engaged couples may be blessed after Mass, at wedding workshops or meetings, at home by parents, or at the wedding rehearsal.

Another possible setting for the blessing might be a regularly occurring gathering of engaged couples after Mass, perhaps monthly or quarterly (depending on the size of the parish and the frequency of weddings). Such a setting might enable engaged couples to meet one another, and may serve as a more public ritual for which other members of the parish community might participate. The order of blessing could also be used at a more formal or structured gathering of engaged couples, either at a Marriage preparation formation session or a wedding liturgy workshop. An opportunity for fellowship may precede or follow the blessing. The blessing may also be presided over by parents at home.

The order of blessing provides rubrics, texts, and gestures specific for a lay presider, and also takes the form of a brief service of the Word, which normally includes a Scripture reading and a psalm. The proclamation of Scripture follows a greeting and introduction to the blessing. Two options for the greeting are provided, one for the ordained and a second for a lay presider. Ordained presiders may also select greetings as found in the Order of Mass from *The Roman Missal*. The choice of Scripture texts includes readings from both the Old and New Testaments, including passages from the Gospel accounts. Suggested passages are provided in the ritual text. There is no Gospel Acclamation if the Gospel is proclaimed. A family member or friend of the couple may proclaim the reading, as indicated by the rubric: "[O]ne of those present or the minister reads a text of Sacred Scripture."[182] The rite suggests that the person presiding "may briefly address those present, shedding light on the biblical reading, so that they may understand with faith the meaning of the celebration and may be able to distinguish it

---

182 OCM, 225.

correctly from the celebration of Marriage."[183] Then, after prayers of intercession, the minister offers the blessing of the couple. Two forms of the blessing
are provided: one to be given by a priest or deacon, and the other by a layperson. A priest or deacon prays with their hands extended whereas a lay
person prays with hands joined. A simple invocation, to which the people
respond, "Amen," concludes the rite:

> May the God of love and peace
> dwell within you,
> direct your steps,
> and strengthen your hearts in his love.[184]

Optional elements include the blessing and exchange of some symbolic
gifts or rings as a sign of the couple's engagement (following the intercessions), and the use of music (a chant at the conclusion of the rite). A blessing
is provided for the exchange of gifts or rings. Parish musicians (especially a
cantor) could be scheduled to lead the psalm and the concluding song.
Consider providing a worship aid for the blessing.

At a more formal blessing that takes place in the church, the couple(s)
can be seated with others in the pews closest to the sanctuary. The assembly
can remain seated during the reading(s) and the priest (or deacon) may invite
the couple(s) to come forward for the blessing itself. The assembly may stand
during the Introductory Rites, the Intercessions, the Blessing, and the
Concluding Rite.

Wedding Liturgy Workshops

It is of great benefit to engaged couples
to participate in a seminar, workshop,
or preparation session related to the
Celebration of Matrimony. Other
components of Marriage preparation
or "Pre-Cana" address the spiritual,

> Both musicians and pastors should make
> every effort to assist couples to
> understand and share in the planning of
> their marriage Liturgy.
>
> —*Sing to the Lord: Music in Divine Worship*, 218

theological, pastoral, and practical aspects of Marriage, many of which are
more focused on the relationship and life of the couple after they are married. A presentation or workshop led by the clergy, the parish liturgical coordinator, or the pastoral musician/director of music provides the opportunity

---

183 OCM, 229.
184 OCM, 235.

to help couples understand the nature of the Sacred Liturgy in order that they may appreciate and respect the structure and the individual elements as they enter into the process of preparation for their wedding liturgy. This liturgical catechesis serves to better prepare a couple to enter into their own wedding with a spirit of "full, conscious, and active participation."[185] If a couple is new to or is otherwise unfamiliar with the parish, perhaps a tour of the parish facilities, especially the church and all the spaces that will be used for the Celebration of Marriage, such as the sacristy or a bride's room, will be helpful for the couple and serve as a gesture of hospitality.

In small parishes or in other communities in which the number of weddings celebrated makes a regularly scheduled group session unfeasible or impractical, then the priest, deacon, or the pastoral musician should devote some time to discussion of the liturgy before simply handing preparation materials to the engaged couple.

After words of welcome and introduction, the presenter should set the context of the conversation by speaking about the nature and purpose of liturgical prayer as an act of worship rather than merely a showcase of fashions, decorations, and the background for an "event." Discuss the role of the liturgical assembly, its importance within the Celebration of Matrimony (rather than merely the bride and groom) and the call to full, conscious, and active participation in the celebration of the rite. Outline the primary components of the liturgy: words (Scripture, prayer, acclamation, dialogue, and so on), silence, gesture and posture, symbol and sign, ritual, and music. Offer some explanation of the notion of "sacramentality" and the way in which sign and symbol embody and communicate deeper realities. Use the Eucharist, particularly Sunday Mass, as the means to illustrate the above points, and then set the context of the Sacrament of Matrimony within the larger context of the liturgy as the "source and summit of the christian life."[186] While the theology of Marriage should be discussed as part of the formal Marriage preparation program, offer a basic summary and illustrate how the theology of the sacrament is manifest in the Celebration of Matrimony itself. The relationship between Eucharist and Marriage should also be emphasized in order to underscore the value of celebrating Marriage within Mass. Pope Francis' apostolic exhortation *Amoris laetitia* expresses the importance of seeing Marriage above all as a sacramental encounter:

---

185 CSL, 14.
186 LG, 11; CSL, 10.

"In their preparation for marriage, the couple should be encouraged to make the liturgical celebration a profound personal experience and to appreciate the meaning of each of its signs. In the case of two baptized persons, the commitment expressed by the words of consent and the bodily union that consummates the marriage can only be seen as signs of the covenantal love and union between the incarnate Son of God and his Church."[187]

Depending on timing and local procedures, couples may have already received preparation materials and thus be familiar with the structure of the Celebration of Matrimony. It is nonetheless important to outline in detail the structure, highlighting the function of each element and the couple's role in preparing the liturgy. Offer suggestions for how to go about choosing the Scripture readings, the prayers, blessings, and other elements. Present a model of "best practices" for the Entrance Procession along with an explanation of the significance of ritual. [188] Include a helpful explanation of why other practices such as a procession centered on the bride alone or keeping the couple separated before the liturgy do not contribute in a positive way to the celebration of the Sacrament of Matrimony.

The director of music or other pastoral musician should offer an explanation of the function and purpose of music within the liturgy and clarify what is understood as "sacred music" or "liturgical music."[189] Emphasis should be given to the "hierarchy" of music for the liturgy: proper texts set to music such as the Responsorial Psalm and the Entrance and Communion Antiphons;[190] the Gloria; acclamations such as the Gospel Acclamation, the optional acclamation within the Celebration of Matriony, and the acclamations of the Eucharistic Prayer; the canticle or hymn of praise at the conclusion of the Celebration of Matrimony; and finally music to accompany the processions. Discuss the three-fold judgement for selecting music (liturgical, pastoral, and musical[191]) and illustrate how

> In their preparation for marriage, the couple should be encouraged to make the liturgical celebration a profound personal experience and to appreciate the meaning of each of its signs.
>
> —*Amoris laetitia*, 123

---

187 *Amoris laetitia* (AL), 213.
188 Refer to page 33 for examples.
189 See chapter III (Music of Catholic Worship) and articles 216 to 224 (Marriage) in *Sing to the Lord: Music in Divine Worship*.
190 Or other appropriate chants in keeping with GIRM, 48 and 87.
191 See STL, 126–136.

The wedding rehearsal is an opportunity to teach the couple and those present about the significance and symbolism of the various parts of the wedding liturgy.

it applies to the particular musical elements of the Celebration of Matrimony. A presentation on music might include the distribution of a list of suggested pieces of music for each element of the Celebration of Matrimony.

Depending on circumstances, the director of music or pastoral musician could offer a demonstration of some pieces of music, could distribute a preview CD (or USB storage device) with options from which to choose, or direct the couple to links on YouTube or the websites of Catholic music publishers. If possible, a cantor may be present to assist in presenting options, especially in regard to the Responsorial Psalm and the acclamations of the rite. Particular attention should be given to the hymn or song of praise following the blessing and giving of the rings within the Celebration of Matrimony. Musicians should be prepared to answer questions about the use of secular music in a way that is both respectful of couples and in accordance with liturgical norms.[192] In a public or group session, consistency is essential; when one exception is granted, then others will likely be requested.

Discussion of approved adaptations and other optional elements should take into consideration any polices of the parish or of the local diocese. Adaptations should be presented in accord with the norms of the rubrics. A brief explanation of the history and significance of the approved adaptations

192 See STL, chapter III.

(the blessing and exchange of the *arras* [coins], the blessing and giving of the *lazo* [cord] or veil) will be helpful in order to situate them within their cultural context. Pastors should determine in advance how to handle the question of other commonly used but unsanctioned adaptations such as the unity candle. It is better not to mention those "unofficial" optional elements unless a couple specifically asks about them. It is important to offer a consistent response that is in accord with parish or diocesan policies and the integrity of the liturgy.

Wedding Rehearsal

The wedding rehearsal is first and foremost a catechetical moment. On a practical level the rehearsal will assure (as much as possible, anyway) the orderly and dignified celebration of the wedding itself, but it is also a "teachable moment" that can invite those in attendance to a more conscious participation. Those who lead the rehearsal should consider not just organizing and practicing with the bridal party and those fulfilling liturgical roles, but teaching about the significance of the various elements of the rite. Consider having a team of parishioners to offer hospitality: perhaps sponsor couples from Marriage preparation sessions or representatives from various liturgical ministries who can assist those who will serve as readers or servers. Some parishes have trained "wedding coordinators" to assist with the various elements of the rehearsal.

Begin the rehearsal with words of welcome and prayer. Consider closing the rehearsal with a blessing for the bride and groom.[193] Words of welcome could include sharing some information about the parish. Keep in mind that many of those in attendance are visitors to the parish, and some might be unfamiliar with the Catholic Church. This is a moment of evangelization! Some parishes offer the opportunity for the Sacrament of Reconciliation after the rehearsal as a means of preparation to celebrate the Sacrament of Matrimony.

The Worship Aid

An effective printed worship aid is one that will facilitate the active participation of the liturgical assembly in the rites being celebrated. To be effective it should include accurate information about the structure and order of the

---

193 See page 77.

celebration as well as music to be sung by the assembly (or page references in a hymnal). In some cases it will be helpful to include the texts of any responses that may be unfamiliar to the assembly (for instance, if a significant number of those in attendance are not Catholic), especially the new dialogue after the reception of the consent in the Celebration of Matrimony.[194]

As a catechetical aid, the parish might consider drafting brief pastoral commentaries to help explain the significance of the various elements of the ritual. Such texts will serve to invite prayerful and conscious participation by the assembly in the wedding rather than merely to presume their passive attendance as spectators. Parishes may also wish to offer assistance with the preparation of a worship aid, including providing music for inclusion under a parish reprint license and appropriate reproducible artwork.[195]

Developing Parish Guidelines

Most parishes provide a brochure about the Marriage preparation process that includes parish policies. This is often presented to couples at the time of their initial inquiry. It is important to recognize the impact of the message that is communicated by the "wedding brochure." Does it communicate a sense of welcome, encouragement, and celebration? Or does it only list restrictions, requirements, and fees? The presentation of policies and procedures is important, and clearly noting the parish's expectations will make matters easier during the process of preparation. However, at the same time these documents set a tone and give the couple an impression of the parish community. The following may be helpful in developing or revising a set of guidelines in a Marriage brochure.

1. Welcome and congratulatory note from the pastor and the pastoral staff

The first words a couple reads should be words of encouragement. The brochure embodies the pastoral approach of Marriage ministry in written form.

2. Brief explanation of the theology of the Sacrament of Matrimony

This explanation illustrates why the Church takes so seriously the process of Marriage preparation.

---

194 See OCM, 65.

195 The sample worship aid on pages 92 and 93 shows a two page spread. Note the headings, music, and catechetical explanations of the different parts of the liturgy; see also STL, 224.

3. Outline of the process of Marriage preparation and its various elements

Explain that the process focuses both on preparing for the Celebration of Matrimony and living a healthy and holy married life.

4. Scheduling the Wedding

Outline the parish's normal times for celebrating weddings. Saturday? Friday evening? What about at a Sunday Mass? What is the schedule for rehearsals? Allow adequate time for travel and arrival for all involved, especially on weeknights.

5. Officiant (Celebrant) for the Wedding

How is the priest or deacon assigned to officiate? Is there a policy regarding priests from outside the parish? How is the Marriage preparation process and the collection of documentation handled when a priest or deacon from outside the parish is invited to officiate? Provide information about how a priest or deacon from outside the parish requests and receives delegation to officiate. In accordance with diocesan norms, a priest or deacon from outside the diocese should request and submit a "letter of suitability" from his diocese or religious order.

6. Documentation

Outline what is required: newly issued baptismal certificates, letters of permission (if the spouses are from other parishes), witness forms, and a premarital questionnaire (investigation). Outline the conditions and process for obtaining dispensations or permissions. Offer helpful information regarding how and where to obtain the marriage license, including timing, process, and fees. Include contact information for the license bureau or courthouse.

7. Information about Marriage preparation (Pre-Cana)

Provide basic information about requirements and options as well as details about registration. Offer an explanation about the purpose and goals of Marriage preparation.

8. Bridal Party

Offer a brief description of the various roles to be filled. Is there a local policy regarding witnesses? Does the parish have guidelines about the number of attendants in the bridal party? Is there a limitation based on space? Consider a policy regarding the minimum age of children who may participate as "ring bearer" or "flower girl" (a good rule of thumb is five years old in order to participate in the procession).

9. Liturgical Ministers

Outline the various liturgical roles to be filled such as readers, servers, extraordinary ministers of Holy Communion, and greeters. What are the requirements to fulfill such roles, and what training or assistance is provided by the parish?

10. Outline of policies

- Photography/videography: Location of photographers, access to balconies or the sanctuary, use of flash, and so on. Is there a policy regarding live streaming of the liturgy? What infrastructure does the parish have for video recording or streaming?

- Flowers: Guidelines and helpful suggestions as to size and location of flower arrangements. Can flowers or bows be attached to pews or doors? What does the parish provide (stands, pedestals, and so on)? Explain the impact of the liturgical time or season. Do flower arrangements need to be removed after a wedding, or do they remain at the church as an offering for use throughout the weekend?

- Use of rice, birdseed, confetti, or bubbles: note the environmental and animal concerns with rice, as well as possible safety hazards. Consider the challenge of clean-up, especially during busy times when there might be multiple weddings on the same day. Offer alternatives if possible.

- Cleanliness: Is there a custodian or sacristan to clean up, or should couples assure that items such as worship aids or flower boxes are gathered and removed after the wedding?

- Use of alcohol and tobacco: Offer a reminder of the dignity and sacredness of the liturgy, and the need especially for the bride and groom's capacity (that is, sobriety) for the valid exchange of consent.

- Dress Code: Due to the dignity and sacredness of the liturgical space and the liturgical celebration, offer suggestions regarding appropriate dress for those who will have a role in the liturgy, including the bride and groom, the bridal party, and those who will exercise a liturgical role.

- Sanctuary Furnishings: Is there a standard arrangement of seating for the bride and groom and other members of the bridal party?

What about the use of kneelers? Mention should be made of the sacredness of the space and the importance of the primary furnishings (altar, ambo, chair for the celebrant, tabernacle, and font) and any limitations on the arrangements of sanctuary furnishings.

11. Worship aids

Offer an explanation of the importance of a printed worship aid to facilitate and encourage active participation in the liturgy. Consider offering a sample worship aid (perhaps a generic model or extra copies of programs from previous weddings that meet the standards and expectations of the parish). Does the parish offer assistance in preparing or printing a worship aid? If not, couples should submit a draft for approval to assure the inclusion and accuracy of necessary information. If the parish makes use of projection screens, outline the procedures for their usage.

12. Banns of Marriage

Explain the history and custom of Banns of Marriage and the importance of sharing information about Marriage with the parish community. What information needs to be gathered? Does another parish need to be notified regarding the publication of banns?

13. Fees

While this is a delicate issue, there are legitimate expenses to be covered, and fees should be clearly outlined so as to avoid misunderstandings. Is there a standard offering for the Church? What are the fees for the sacristan, parish wedding coordinator, or other liturgical ministers? Is there a customary or suggested offering ("stole fee") for the priest or deacon?[196] How are fees for pastoral musicians handled? Is a "bench fee" collected for the Director of Music when a musician from outside the parish is hired for a wedding? [197] On the other hand, if a couple understands the sacramental nature of Marriage and the importance of the liturgical celebration, could the parish consider not charging any fees? If so, compensation for musicians and other employees must be considered.

---

196 Consult the norms or compensation guidelines of the local diocese for any policies regarding stipends and stole fees.

197 Pastors should be familiar with compensation guidelines and standards provided by the National Association of Pastoral Musicians (www.NPM.org) and the American Guild of Organists (www.agohq.org). Contract or employment agreements for directors of music should outline in detail the fee structure for weddings.

Other Pastoral Considerations

Each couple and individual is unique, and there are undoubtedly unique pastoral situations that arise in preparation for the Celebration of Matrimony. These, too, should be handled with care and concern for the couple and their families but also with respect for the Sacred Liturgy and the dignity of the Sacrament of Matrimony. It is important during the Marriage preparation process to learn not only about the bride and groom but about their families as well. What they witnessed and experienced about Marriage—for better or worse—as they were growing up will undoubtedly have an effect on their own Marriage. Understanding their families will also help to prepare for the Celebration of Matrimony. For example, it would be helpful to know if the parents of the bride and groom were themselves living healthy Marriages that can be pointed out or celebrated during the wedding (perhaps during the homily) or if there were divorces and remarriages among the parents or grandparents. Some of these situations require great pastoral sensitivity even in regard to the arrangement of seating for parents and family.

If one or both of the parties has been married before and are approaching the Church to marry following an annulment, there are additional pastoral circumstances to consider. There may be children from a prior marriage who could be incorporated in some way into the ceremony. One might consider offering a blessing of the family, as found in the *Book of Blessings*, at the rehearsal or at the reception, or simply to acknowledge the presence of children.[198]

Oftentimes the priest or deacon is invited to offer an invocation or to bless the meal at the wedding rehearsal dinner and/or the wedding reception. One might also consider inviting the bride and groom to lead the prayer before the meal at the reception, and to assist them in preparing the prayer in advance. What an example of a holy Marriage it would be to have the newly married couple share in a moment of prayer together!

Pastoral Care and Support for Married Couples: "Post-Cana"

The *Rite of Christian Initiation of Adults* includes the period of mystagogy, the time after the celebration of the sacraments of initiation, to allow for deeper reflection on the mysteries just celebrated. Unfortunately this model tends not to carry over to the celebration of other sacraments. Too often after

---

198 The Order for the Blessing of a Family is found in chapter 1 of the *Book of Blessings*.

the Marriage liturgy, the newly married couple "disappears" from the Church. Certainly in some cases the couple relocates to another parish or another city or town. Parishes should consider what kinds of pastoral outreach and support are provided for the recently married. A "post-Cana" program could simply include gatherings for young couples as a way to strengthen their connections to the parish community, but gatherings could include time for reflection and prayer. Perhaps a recently married couple could be invited to participate in the pre-Cana process as a witness and example.

The Order of Celebrating Matrimony includes the Order of Blessing a Married Couple within Mass on the Anniversary of Marriage.[199] Parishes could reach out to couples on the first anniversary of their Marriage in order to arrange a time to offer the blessing solely to them. Otherwise, many parishes hold a monthly celebration for the anniversary of Marriage (for those married during that particular month). Consider sending a note to couples on the first anniversary of their Marriage to invite them to participate. Perhaps it will instill in them the desire to participate annually.

Marriage and Evangelization

In *Amoris laetitia*, Pope Francis reminds pastors of the importance of the role of the assembly in the Celebration of Matrimony and the opportunity for evangelization:

[W]e are promoters of the culture of encounter. We are living sacraments of the embrace between God's riches and our poverty. We are witnesses of the abasement and the condescension of God who anticipates in love our every response.

—Pope Francis, "Address to Bishops of the United States at St. Matthew's Cathedral," September 23, 2015

"The marriage liturgy is a unique event, which is both a family and a community celebration. The first signs of Jesus were performed at the wedding feast of Cana. The good wine, resulting from the Lord's miracle that brought joy to the beginning of a new family, is the new wine of Christ's covenant with the men and women of every age. . . . Frequently, the celebrant speaks to a congregation that includes people who seldom participate in the life of the Church, or who are members of other Christian denominations or religious

---

199 See appendix III of the OCM (237–251); see also page 103

communities. The occasion thus provides a valuable opportunity to proclaim the Gospel of Christ."[200]

How the celebrant invites people to experience the fullness of the mystery being celebrated can go a long way to aid the work of evangelization. The assembly should be encouraged to full participation. A printed worship aid, an effective cantor or leader of song, and brief invitations or explanations by the celebrant,[201] can be used effectively in this regard.

Good Marriage preparation encourages couples to a deeper participation in the life of the Church.

Ministry to engaged couples is often complicated. It necessarily involves many facets: pastoral care, faith formation and catechesis, evangelization, hospitality, Canon Law, liturgical preparation, counseling, and spiritual direction. Because of this, clergy, pastoral musicians, and formation ministers frequently take on many roles during this process. Adding to all of this is the pressure that, for many couples, Marriage preparation is the only close and personal contact they have had with the Church in many years. This experience will either encourage them to a more active participation in the life of the Church or set them at even further distance from it.

The *Catechism of the Catholic Church* suggests that the sacraments of the Church have the capacity to nourish and nurture faith:

> "The purpose of the sacraments is to sanctify men, to build up the Body of Christ and, finally, to give worship to God. Because they are signs they also instruct. They not only presuppose faith, but by words and objects they also nourish, strengthen, and express it. That is why they are called 'sacraments of *faith*.'"[202]

200 AL, 216; see also *Relatio finalis*, 59.
201 See GIRM, 31.
202 *Catechism of the Catholic Church*, 1123; quoting CSL, 59.

The Church's ministry to engaged couples must demonstrate a willingness to offer generously the gift of God's grace as a help and a means of growing in holiness rather than merely a reward for faithful adherence to policies, procedures, and teaching. As Pope Francis teaches in *Evangelii gaudium*:

"Everyone can share in some way in the life of the Church; everyone can be part of the community, nor should the doors of the sacraments be closed for simply any reason. This is especially true of the sacrament which is itself "the door": baptism. The Eucharist, although it is the fullness of sacramental life, is not a prize for the perfect but a powerful medicine and nourishment for the weak. These convictions have pastoral consequences that we are called to consider with prudence and boldness. Frequently, we act as arbiters of grace rather than its facilitators. But the Church is not a tollhouse; it is the house of the Father, where there is a place for everyone, with all their problems."[203]

Pope Francis, in his address to the Bishops of the United States during his Pastoral Visit in September, 2015, reflected on the challenge of facing difficult pastoral situations. He stated:

"I know that you face many challenges, and that the field in which you sow is unyielding and that there is always the temptation to give in to fear, to lick one's wounds, to think back on bygone times and to devise harsh responses to fierce opposition.

And yet we are promoters of the culture of encounter. We are living sacraments of the embrace between God's riches and our poverty. We are witnesses of the abasement and the condescension of God who anticipates in love our every response."[204]

It is easy to lament a lack of enthusiasm or understanding among couples who are not as interested in the process of Marriage preparation as one would hope. Pope Francis suggests, however, that harsh rules or processes weighed down with burdens are not the answer. An inviting approach will promote an encounter with the Lord, and that encounter has the power to open the hearts of the couple on their way to the Sacrament of Matrimony.

---

203 EG, 47.

204 Pope Francis, "Address to Bishops of the United States at St. Matthew's Cathedral," September 23, 2015; available from http://w2.vatican.va/content/francesco/en/speeches/2015/september/documents/papa-francesco_20150923_usa-vescovi.html; accessed October 1, 2015.

THE INTRODUCTORY RITES

In the Roman Catholic Church, the bride and groom may process together with their witnesses in the liturgical procession as a sign of their journey and faith in Christ. All are invited to stand and sing the gathering song while the procession takes place. This begins the Introductory Rites which prepare our hearts and minds for worship.

GATHERING SONG

When Love Is Found
Brian Wren

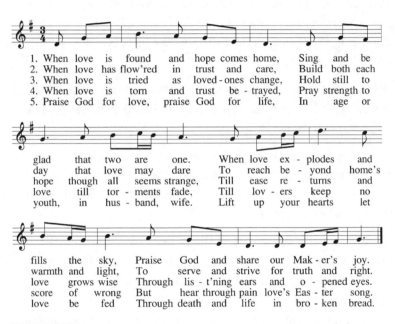

1. When love is found and hope comes home, Sing and be glad that two are one. When love ex-plodes and fills the sky, Praise God and share our Mak-er's joy.
2. When love has flow'red in trust and care, Build both each day that love may dare To reach be-yond home's warmth and light, To serve and strive for truth and right.
3. When love is tried as loved-ones change, Hold still to hope though all seems strange, Till ease re-turns and love grows wise Through lis-t'ning ears and o-pened eyes.
4. When love is torn and trust be-trayed, Pray strength to love till tor-ments fade, Till lov-ers keep no score of wrong But hear through pain love's Eas-ter song.
5. Praise God for love, praise God for life, In age or youth, in hus-band, wife. Lift up your hearts let love be fed Through death and life in bro-ken bread.

Text: Brian Wren, b.1936
Tune: O WALY WALY, LM; English; harm. by Martin West, b.1929
© 1983, Hope Publishing Co.

This is a sample spread for how a worship aid may be formatted. Note the catechetical explanations that have been added. Proper music credits should also be added. Consider adding all music credits to the next to last page of the worship aid (reserving the back cover as a blank page or as a place for art). Music: *Mass of the Angels and Saints*, Steven R. Janco, © 1996, 2010,

THE SIGN OF THE CROSS AND GREETING

Catholics begin and end liturgical prayer in the name of the Trinity; our Christian life gives witness to the relationship of Father, Son, and Holy Spirit.

Priest: In the name of the Father, and of the Son,
and of the Holy Spirit.

All: **Amen.**

Priest: The grace of our Lord Jesus Christ,
and the love of God,
and the communion of the Holy Spirit
be with you all.

All: **And with your spirit.**

OPENING ADDRESS

With joy, the priest addresses the couple and all present to prepare them inwardly for the celebration of Matrimony.

THE GLORIA

Mass of the Angels and Saints
Steven R. Janco

The Gloria is the great song of the angels. We give praise to God for his glory and salvation in Christ. The cantor will intone the refrain and all are invited to respond in song. The refrain is repeated after each stanza of the hymn.

We praise you,
we bless you,
we adore you,
we glorify you,
we give you thanks for your great glory,
Lord God, heavenly King,
O God, almighty Father. **R.**

Frequently Asked Questions

1. How are parish weddings an opportunity for evangelization? How can parish staff members help couples find a home in the Church?

First and foremost, pastoral leaders must begin by recognizing that ministry to couples preparing for Marriage is in fact an opportunity for evangelization. Often a couple's inquiry regarding the celebration of their Marriage is their first personal contact with the Church in many years. Even couples who attend Mass regularly might know very little about processes, policies, and expectations. Many couples who seek to be married in the Church are not regularly attending Mass, but they presume to want to be married in the Church because of their own roots. Sometimes, however, couples approach

Preparing couples for Marriage is a ministry of evangelization.

the Church at the urging of parents or grandparents. In any case, the Church needs to welcome couples in the spirit of Jesus Christ.

Think about first impressions: What happens when a prospective bride or groom calls to inquire about a wedding? Who takes the call or responds to the e-mail, and what message does that response send? A couple greeted only by a list of rules, requirements, or a litany of nos, will not likely feel welcomed. Established polices are necessary, especially in large parishes accustomed to celebrating many weddings each year, but initial contact with a couple should send a message of welcome, support, and joy before furnishing any guidelines or checklists.

2. Sacraments are public rituals of the Church. How can weddings be a celebration of the whole parish?

It is rare to see Marriage celebrated at a Sunday Mass in a parish because cultural expectations and custom simply have not fostered that practice (and this is not limited to Catholicism). Still, parishes might consider promoting this practice at least as a way to demonstrate the primacy of Sunday as the fitting place for the celebration of many of the rites of the Church. Even when Marriage is celebrated at a time other than Sunday, the celebration is still part of the Sacred Liturgy and is therefore part of the public prayer of the Church. Involvement of various liturgical ministers from the parish community, or the invitation for parishioners to attend the liturgical celebration might strengthen the couple's connection to the community in this way.

Of particular importance in the celebration of Marriage is the ministry of hospitality. Weddings normally bring many visitors to a parish, and while members of the bridal party, parents, and sometimes even the bride and groom are there to greet their guests when they arrive, having someone to serve as a parish "host" or greeter (in addition to a sacristan or parish wedding coordinator) can help facilitate guests in finding their way around, and they can troubleshoot small problems that may arise such as unlocking a locked door, turning on a light, or pointing the way to an accessible

Hospitality is essential for the celebration of Marriage.

entrance. Attentiveness to the good order and cleanliness of facilities and simply having the space prepared in a timely fashion shows that the parish is welcoming, organized, and ready for the celebration.

Parishes might consider the role that the "sponsor couple" who assisted with the couple's formation could play in the Celebration of Matrimony. Perhaps they serve as the ministers of hospitality, or could participate in the liturgy as extraordinary ministers of Holy Communion (if they have been properly trained and commissioned) as a way of accompanying the couple through the preparation process to the celebration of the sacrament.

Acknowledgment of and ongoing support for newly married couples in the day-to-day life of the parish could include social or formational gatherings for couples. Consider some ways to offer congratulations to a newly married couple upon their return from their honeymoon (that is, when they are welcomed back to the Sunday assembly for the first time as husband and wife).

3. In what ways can the whole parish pray for engaged couples?

The traditional practice of announcing or publishing the Banns of Marriage serves as an announcement to the parish of upcoming weddings. While the Banns fulfill a canonical obligation they could also be used as an invitation for prayer for the couples. Parishes could include intentions of the Universal Prayer (Prayer of the Faithful) at weekend Masses for couples married on a particular weekend. Use of the Blessing of Engaged Couples, found in the appendix of *The Order of Celebrating Matrimony*, could be offered after Mass on particular weekends (since the ritual restricts the use of this blessing to occasions outside Mass). Praying with engaged couples at each meeting or gathering is also important. The community is not only praying for them, but the couple is part of the praying community!

4. How can the parish staff be present to couples during the engagement process and after the wedding?

Parishes, and particularly staff members, must recognize that couples preparing for Marriage are in fact members of the community—or at least they could be—and should be treated as parishioners for whom a particular form of pastoral outreach is essential. If couples are perceived as "visitors" or "clients" for whom a service is being provided for a fee, then opportunities for substantial pastoral care will be missed. A good approach begins with helping the couple to see themselves as members of the community, and as such they have something to offer the community and something to receive from the community. Making connections between the couple and the community in the form of notices, cards or notes, or events hosted for soon-to-be or recently-married couples can help foster stronger connections.

5. Weddings are often a source of tension for parish staffs. How can parish staff members build solid relationships with those who are preparing for Marriage? How can we pastorally say no to couples' ideas that are not acceptable for Catholic liturgy?

Good communication and cooperation among all those who work with couples preparing for Marriage is essential. Parish staffs might begin by determining exactly who is involved in "Marriage ministry." Think about everyone who has contact with the couple, including receptionists or administrative assistants who are often the first point of contact and who answer many questions before a couple meets with the priest or deacon who will officiate. Consider a gathering of everyone involved—administrative assistants, sacristans, music ministers, clergy, and adult faith formation ministers or those who coordinate the Marriage preparation process (for example, Pre-Cana class, sponsor couples, or Engaged Encounter)—in order to assure consistent application of policies as well as to establish a welcoming approach to couples from the moment of their first inquiry.

It is the lack of understanding on the part of both liturgists (especially clergy officiants and pastoral musicians) and couples preparing for Marriage that often leads to tension during the preparation process. One could begin the conversation about the wedding liturgy with some basic principles about the nature of the liturgy as an action of the Church, an act of worship, and about the nature of the Eucharist (in the case of a Nuptial Mass) as an act of praise and thanks to God. This would help the couple to appreciate certain restrictions and also see other attractive possibilities. Saying no must also include alternative choices that lead to a stronger yes. It is not as though this process needs to be about compromise, but one cannot always say no without offering something of a yes.

6. Couples often have preconceived ideas for how weddings should be celebrated. These ideas often directly contradict the Church's rituals. In what ways can the Church be better at preparing couples with a sense of Catholic liturgy?

The easy and short answer to this question is always "catechesis," but this is, of course, easier said than done. Parishes cannot expect couples to come with a healthy understanding of the Sacrament of Matrimony and an appreciation for good liturgical practice unless these are taught and fostered in every aspect of parish life. Faith formation programs must have as their aim not merely teaching doctrinal concepts but also cultivating a living faith in the hearts of believers in such a way that their choices, in this case regarding Marriage, are shaped by the traditions, customs, and practices of the Church.[1]

7. Parish staff members are just as guilty of promoting the "venue" model as couples are with their misunderstanding of the Church as "just another venue." How can parish staff members move beyond the notion of the "wedding business"?

There is a difference between an effective and efficient pastoral plan for ministry with couples preparing for Marriage and a wedding policy for conducting the "wedding business." Especially in large parishes accustomed to hosting many weddings each year there are elements of ministry that can be "standardized" without appearing cold or impersonal. Some parishes host large-group gatherings of couples to offer presentations on liturgical music as a prelude to an official one-on-one preparation session with the pastoral musician or liturgist. Policies and procedures are important, but such guidelines must be grounded in a desire to offer pastoral care for the couples rather than merely to avoid any personal contact with couples. Guidelines should communicate a desire to share in the sacramental moment rather than merely communicate a list of prohibitions, restrictions, and fees.

---

1 See OCM, 14 which states: "Pastors of souls must take care that in their own community this assistance is provided especially: 1) by preaching, by catechesis adapted to children, young people, and adults, and through means of social communication, so that the Christian faithful are instructed about the meaning of Christian Marriage and about the role of Christian spouses and parents."

The matter of fees raises many questions. There are expenses related to Marriage preparation and the celebration of Marriage, but should the parish charge a fee for the celebration of a sacrament? This is obviously a larger question that also applies to the celebration of Baptism, First Eucharist, and Confirmation. Parishes would not normally charge a fee for the Rite of Christian Initiation of Adults, and yet fees for other sacraments are more commonplace. Compensation for sacristans, parish wedding coordinators, and pastoral musicians could be addressed in other ways as a means of streamlining the costs imposed on couples. Offering the services of the parish as a form of outreach and ministry rather than a

Parish communities should be welcoming and pray for engaged couples.

service to be rendered for a fee could send a strong message to couples about the nature of the process as a sacred encounter rather than a transaction.

8. As a liturgical minister in the Church, I notice that many couples are not expecting me to minister to them. Instead, they see my role as one of many boxes to check off on their "to do list." How can I be more ministerial in my approach?

Preparing for the wedding liturgy must include more than simply the list of check boxes on a preparation sheet. If the couple is given the opportunity to participate in the preparation process (as they should!), then some guidance ought to be provided regarding the nature of liturgy and the functions and purposes of the various parts of the liturgy before delving into a list of choices of texts, rituals, and music. In order for this to be effective ministry, the attitude of all involved—staff as well as volunteers—must be that of an opportunity for service and pastoral care rather than a burden or an intrusion. Whenever a minister (priest or deacon, pastoral musician, or parish wedding coordinator) meets with a couple, always begin with prayer. This is less about business than it is about an encounter with the Lord.

9. How can parish staff members be more sensitive to interfaith or mixed Marriages? How are the differences addressed liturgically?

Every couple is unique, so it stands to reason that each wedding we celebrate will have its own unique circumstances. Marriages between a Catholic and a baptized Christian of another denomination or between a Catholic and an unbaptized person present additional situations that call for pastoral sensitivity. Understanding not only similarities and differences between various Christian communities and other faiths will be helpful, but it is also important to be sensitive to attitudes of families and how knowledgeable they are about their own faith and the customs of the Catholic Church. One must keep in mind what the various elements of the Marriage Rite signify and how they might be perceived by those of another faith tradition. For example, while many couples might be interested in making a devotional act to the Blessed Virgin Mary by placing flowers before an image of her, that ritual makes little sense coming from a couple with no devotion to Mary, especially if the bride herself is not Catholic (since this ritual tends to focus more on the bride's offering to Mary). On the other hand, this ritual could be a moment to nurture or encourage devotion if there is proper catechesis to prepare the couple for it.

Normally a Marriage between a Catholic and a baptized Christian takes place at a ceremony outside Mass, but there may be occasions when it might be appropriate to celebrate a Nuptial Mass in this context. In that case, great care must be taken to encourage the unity of the spouses even though the non-Catholic spouse does not share in Communion.

10. Couples often include family and friends as liturgical ministers. As a parish, how do I ensure they carry out their ministries properly and according to our customs?

If couples are invited to choose individuals to serve in liturgical ministries, they should be informed about parish practices, diocesan polices, and liturgical norms. Discussion of the particular functions and the necessary qualifications for ministers is important. Choosing someone to proclaim the Scripture readings, for instance, should be done with the goal of effective proclamation rather than merely to honor a friend who was not included in the bridal party. Diocesan norms and liturgical laws might limit who can serve as an extraordinary minister of Holy Communion (even if someone is to be deputized for a particular occasion).

In order to support the effective ministry of these volunteers, the parish must do its part to provide the necessary resources and support. Those who work with engaged couples should see that those who are chosen to function as readers receive copies of the texts they are to proclaim (Scripture readings or intentions of the Universal Prayer/Prayer of the Faithful) in advance so that they can adequately prepare to serve. The parish should also consider how training could be provided not only by the priest or deacon but by ministry coordinators, which would also serve to connect these ministers to those of the parish community. For instance, a parish wedding coordinator could also be trained to assist those who will serve as readers, servers, or extraordinary ministers of Holy Communion so that their training is distinct from the wedding rehearsal with the bridal party.

11. How can I ensure best practice for the liturgical rites? Assistance with worship aids? Preparing liturgical binders? Using the Lectionary instead of sheets of paper? Appropriate music?

Assuring good liturgical practice begins with seeing the Celebration of Matrimony as part of the liturgical life of the parish even though (or especially because) the majority of participants might be visitors or non-churchgoers. Every effort should be made to maintain consistency with the everyday procedures and customs of the parish. Use of parish ministers for ministries such as servers, sacristans, and ministers of hospitality will provide structural support. For example, if the Entrance Procession at Sunday Mass is led by a crossbearer, then the same

If the Entrance Procession at Sunday Mass is led by a crossbearer, do so at a wedding.

should occur at the Entrance Procession of the wedding liturgy. In regard to liturgical music, use of repertoire consistent with that of the Sunday assembly, especially for responses and acclamations, will provide another point of connection. The parish could take on the responsibility of producing worship aids (or arranging for projection of music if that is the practice) for weddings to reflect the consistency of the rituals.

The use of signs and symbols should not be minimized for the sake of convenience. Proper use of liturgical books, including the *Lectionary for Mass* (rather than photocopied sheets of paper) and the *Book of the Gospels* (rather than the ritual book for Marriage) for the Scripture readings communicates the importance of the Word of God. The blessing and exchange of rings should communicate a sense of respect for the rings themselves. If there is to be a ring bearer, then the actual rings should be borne in the procession rather than a facsimile thereof. Keeping in mind the primary sign of the couple themselves should be a priority. If incense is used, then the couple could be incensed after the altar, the gifts of bread and wine, and the priest are incensed.

APPENDIX

Preparing the Order of Blessing a Married Couple within Mass on the Anniversary of Marriage

New in the second edition of *The Order of Celebrating Matrimony* is a ritual for blessing couples on the anniversary of their Marriage. While a blessing of couples had been included in the *Book of Blessings*,[1] and most components of the new order of blessing are simply a retranslation of that text, the earlier ritual did not include any form of a renewal of commitment more commonly referred to as "renewal of vows." A blessing of couples on their anniversary in an earlier provisional collection of blessings, the *Liturgikon*, did include a renewal of vows.[2] The option of a renewal of commitment by the couple is a welcome addition to encourage their active participation in the ritual.

Some parishes offer a blessing of married couples during regularly scheduled Masses. Some choose to offer such a blessing at a set time each month (for couples celebrating anniversaries that month), while others may schedule an annual celebration near the time of World Marriage Day (for couples celebrating significant anniversaries such as twenty-five, fifty, or sixty or more years during that year).[3] Pastoral ministers should promote the availability of the blessing for wedding anniversaries, perhaps inviting any couple who celebrates fifty years of Marriage to receive the blessing at a Sunday Mass as a means of giving support and encouragement for healthy Marriages.

The ritual itself envisions a special celebration on the occasion of a couple's significant wedding anniversary with a Mass, making use of proper texts from the Masses and Prayers for Various Needs and Occasions, 11: On

---

1 See *Book of Blessings* (BB), chapter 1, part III.

2 Rev. Walter J Schmitz, ss, and Rev. Terence E. Tierney, eds., *Liturgikon: Pastoral Ministrations* (Huntington, Indiana: Our Sunday Visitor, Inc., 1977), see pp. 97–98.

3 World Marriage Day is celebrated each year on the second Sunday of February.

the Anniversaries of Marriage.[4] Readings may be taken from the Celebration of Matrimony or from the Mass for Giving Thanks to God.[5]

The Mass takes place in the usual way (that is, it follows the prescriptions of *The Roman Missal*). There is no indication given that the married couple is to participate in the Entrance Procession or any preferences provided regarding seating. They could participate in the procession and have a place prepared for them in the sanctuary, or they could remain seated with their family and friends. After the homily, the priest invites the couple to stand and he may invite them to come forward to stand before the altar.

The priest invites the couple to renew their commitment, and he indicates that this is done in a spirit of prayer, which reminds those gathered that the couple's commitment to one another is also a commitment to God:

> **N.** and **N.**,
> on the anniversary of that celebration
> at which you joined your lives in an unbreakable bond
> through the Sacrament of Matrimony,
> you now intend to renew before the Lord
> the promises you made to one another.
> Turn to the Lord in prayer,
> that these vows may be strengthened by divine grace.[6]

The couple may do so quietly or in silence, although there is no indication of how exactly this might take place. The earlier form found in the *Book of Blessings* also prescribed that this "renewal"[7] took place in silence. It is interesting to note that the renewal of commitment is not so much a reiteration of promises (vows) as it is a prayer of thanksgiving for blessings and a prayer seeking God's grace to remain faithful to their Marriage promise:

> *The husband says:*
> Blessed are you, Lord,
> for by your goodness I took **N.** as my wife.
>
> *The wife says:*
> Blessed are you, Lord,
> for by your goodness I took **N.** as my husband.

---

4 OCM, 237; see also *The Roman Missal*, Masses for Various Needs and Occasions, 11, A–C.

5 *Lectionary for Mass*, vol. 4, *Masses for Various Needs and Occassions*.

6 OCM, 240.

7 BB, 96.

Both say:
Blessed are you, Lord,
for in the good and the bad times of our life
you have stood lovingly by our side.
Help us, we pray,
to remain faithful in our love for one another,
so that we may be true witnesses
to the covenant you have made with humankind.[8]

Then the Priest acknowledges their prayer (following the pattern of ritual found in the celebration of Marriage itself) in these words:

May the Lord keep you safe all the days of your life.
May he be your comfort in adversity
and your support in prosperity.
May he fill your home with blessings.
Through Christ our Lord.[9]

The couple may choose to have their rings blessed, although there is no indication that the spouses bestow them again. Rather than bless the rings with holy water as in the Celebration of Matrimony,[10] here the rings may be honored with incense.[11] The ritual in the *Book of Blessings* also prescribed the use of incense. If new rings are to be given, a separate formula of blessing is provided, although again there is no formula provided for the bestowal or giving of rings by the spouses.[12]

The Universal Prayer (Prayer of the Faithful) follows, and a more substantial "prayer in common"[13] is provided as an alternative to the usual form. The intentions take the form of invocations of God the Father asking for particular blessings upon the couple and upon all married couples. This alternate form could be quite effective because of its unique structure and the sentiments and prayers it provides. Note the response, "Renew the fidelity of your servants, Lord."[14]

---

8 OCM, 242.
9 OCM, 242.
10 See OCM 66, 100, 131.
11 OCM, 243.
12 OCM, 244.
13 OCM, 244.
14 OCM, 245.

The Liturgy of the Eucharist takes place as usual. The rubrics encourage the couple to bring up the gifts of bread, wine, and water.[15] A special form of the Nuptial Blessing is provided and it follows the Lord's Prayer. The embolism ("Deliver us, Lord . . .") is omitted as at the Nuptial Mass. The rubric indicates that the priest faces the couple, but does not indicate further whether he leaves the altar to stand near the couple or if he remains at the altar. How this is enacted depends on the arrangement of the sanctuary and where the couple is seated. "After 'The peace of the Lord' has been said, if appropriate, in accordance with local customs, the couple and all others offer one another a sign that suitably expresses peace and charity."[16] The couple may receive both species.

An optional form of Solemn Blessing is included. If a deacon is present, he invites all to "Bow down for the blessing."[17] The priest extends hands over the couple and prays that the Father will "grant [them] his joy," that the Son will "stand by [them] with compassion in good times and in bad" and that the Holy Spirit will "always pour forth his love into [their] hearts."[18] The final blessing is the same adapted form as used during the Celebration of Matrimony.

> And may almighty God bless all of you, who are gathered here,
> the Father, and the Son, ✚ and the Holy Spirit.[19]

This blessing obviously serves as an encouragement and a help to couples as they continue to live in married love. It also provides an opportunity to invite couples to reflect on the blessings they have already experienced in married life. In preparing a couple for this celebration, the priest might suggest that the couple spend some time in reflection on how they have seen God's grace at work in their lives, how they have experienced his love in each other, and how they have come to trust all the more in the Lord's love for them. Such a perspective was not possible on their wedding day, and the "renewal of commitment" on the occasion of their anniversary becomes an expression of their awareness of the effectiveness of God's grace in the Sacrament. Such a reflection could even on occasion be shared with couples preparing for Marriage as part of their Marriage preparation program.

---

15 See OCM, 247.

16 OCM, 249.

17 OCM, 251.

18 OCM, 251.

19 OCM, 251.

RESOURCES

Church Documents and Ritual Books

It is important for all who are involved with preparing wedding liturgies to have access to the liturgical books that are used in the Church's liturgies and sacramental celebrations. They are available from various publishers.

- *Book of Blessings.* This ritual book includes a variety of blessings for various occasions. The introduction is especially helpful and informative regarding the use and purpose of blessings by ordained and lay Catholics. Available from multiple publishers.

- *Catholic Household Blessings & Prayers.* Washington, DC: United States Conference of Catholic Bishops, 2007. A great resource, particularly for use in Catholic homes. It includes a rich collection of basic Catholic prayers as well as blessings for many different life events and stages, as well as blessings related to the Sacrament of Matrimony.

- *Code of Canon Law.* This is the comprehensive book of rules and regulations governing the celebration of the sacraments, the administration of different entities in the Church (that is, parishes and dioceses) and many other aspects of Catholic life—all aimed at the sanctification and salvation of members of the Roman Catholic Church. The chapters on Marriage include pastoral care in preparation for Marriage, impediments and convalidations, along with other issues related to the sacrament. Available from multiple publishers.

- *Lectionary for Mass* (especially vol. 4, *Ritual and Votive Masses*). The complete collection of Scripture readings for the celebration of the Eucharistic liturgy on Sundays and every day of the year. Volume 4 includes the readings recommended for weddings in the Catholic Church. The ritual and study editions are available from LTP.

- *The Liturgy Documents, Volume One: Fifth Edition* and *Volume Two*: 2nd ed. Chicago, IL: Liturgy Training Publications, 2012. These books include all the basic documents needed for anyone involved in liturgy preparation. Those helping couples prepare for the wedding liturgy should be familiar with at least the following documents: *Constitution on the Sacred Liturgy, The General Instruction of the Roman Missal, Universal Norms on the Liturgical Year and the General Roman Calendar, Redemptionis sacramentum, Sing to the Lord: Music in Divine Worship,* and *Built of Living Stones: Art, Architecture and Worship.*

- *The Order of Celebrating Matrimony.* 2nd ed. The recently revised book of prayers, rituals, rubrics, and Scripture readings for the celebration of the Sacrament of Matrimony. There are three options for the celebration of the sacrament: Within Mass; Without Mass; and Between a Catholic and a Catechumen or a Non-Christian. English-only editions are available from Catholic Book Publishing, the United States Conference of Catholic Bishops (USCCB), Ave Maria, and The Liturgical Press; an English and Spanish bilingual edition is available from The Liturgical Press. The editions from The Liturgical Press are also distributed by Liturgy Training Publications.

- *The Roman Missal.* This book includes all the prayers for the celebration of Mass for each day of the year. It also includes all the prayer texts for Ritual Masses (including Matrimony) and other special occasions. Available from multiple publishers including Liturgy Training Publications (chapel and ritual editions).

Theological and Historical Resources

- Cahill, Perry J. *The Mystery of Marriage: A Theology of the Body and the Sacrament.* Chicago, IL: Liturgy Training Publications, 2016. This remarkable study offers a comprehensive explanation of the Catholic Church's teaching on the Sacrament of Matrimony. Incorporating the rich insights found in St. John Paul II's *Theology of the Body,* the author presents a theology of Marriage that incorporates the biblical, systematic, pastoral, and historical traditions which have shaped our understanding of this sacrament.

- Cooke, Bernard. *Sacraments and Sacramentality.* St. Paul, MN: Twenty-Third Publications, 1994. A thoughtful discussion of the sacraments and how they relate to the realities of our everyday lives.

- Lawler, Michael. *Marriage and the Catholic Church: Disputed Questions.* Collegeville, MN: The Liturgical Press, 2002. A frank discussion of many of the contemporary issues facing couples marrying or married in the Church, with historical background and pastoral sensitivity. Topics include models of Marriage in the Catholic Church, friendship in marriage, cohabitation, divorce, remarriage, and the Christian family.

- Martos, Joseph. *Doors to the Sacred: A Historical Introduction to Sacraments in the Catholic Church.* Ligouri, MO: Ligouri Publications, 2014. This lengthy (576 pages!) book is a classic treatise on the historical development of sacraments in the Church. The latest edition has been updated to include recent changes in *The Roman Missal* and includes an informative timeline of sacramental changes through the years.

- Osborne, M. Kenan, OFM. *Sacramental Theology: Fifty Years after Vatican II.* Hobe Sound, FL: Lectio Publishing, 2014. A comprehensive and systematic discussion of how sacramental theology has evolved since the Second Vatican Council.

- Mick, Lawrence. *Understanding the Sacraments Today.* Collegeville, MN: The Liturgical Press, 2006. The chapter on Marriage is a very good overview of the richness of the sacrament in the Catholic Church, with helpful discussion questions at the end of the chapter.

- Stevenson, Kenneth. *To Join Together: The Rite of Marriage (Studies in the Reformed Rites of the Church).* Collegeville, MN: The Liturgical Press, 1987. A historical survey of the development of the Christian Marriage Rites.

- Stice, Randy. *Understanding the Sacraments of Vocation: A Rite-Based Approach.* Chicago, IL: Liturgy Training Publications, 2016. The author offers insightful catechesis on the sacraments of vocation based on the methodology presented in *Sacramentum caritatis*. Guiding readers through the Rites of Orders and Matrimony, the author examines each of the rites' Old Testament foundations, liturgical history, and sacramental theology, exploring the way in which the sacraments of vocation affect and influence one's daily Christian life.

- Thomas, David. *Christian Marriage: The New Challenge*. 2nd ed. Collegeville, Minnesota: The Liturgical Press, 2007. In this book, Thomas discusses the various challenging aspects of Marriage, including sexuality and intimacy, gender equality, and spirituality of the married couple. Also included are chapters on divorce and remarriage, cohabitation, and a theology of Christian family.

Pastoral Resources

- Dooley, Sandra. *A Guide to Catholic Weddings: Q&A for Couples*. Chicago, IL: Liturgy Training Publications, 2016. A collection of questions and answers regarding the Catholic wedding preparation process and the wedding ceremony. Helpful for newly engaged couples as they begin to prepare the many details of their Catholic wedding, this resource will walk them through the process—whom to contact, when to schedule, why the Church expects certain things, and the options for the ceremony.

- *For Your Marriage* (www.ForYourMarriage.org). The United States Bishops provide this website which includes an excellent twenty-two-minute video, "Saying I Do: What Happens at a Catholic Wedding." The website includes up-to-date information, including daily Marriage tips, blogs, and resources for parents and for dating/engaged couples.

- *Marriage: Love and Life in the Divine Plan*. Washington, DC: United States Conference of Catholic Bishops, 2009. This pastoral letter from the United States Bishops presents basic Catholic teaching on Marriage and also discusses various challenges for couples in today's world.

- *A Marriage Sourcebook*. Compiled by J. Robert Baker, Joni Gibley, and Kevin Charles Gibley. Chicago, IL: Liturgy Training Publications, 1994. An anthology of Scripture, prayer, poetry, fiction, hymn texts, and even a bit of humor regarding the joys and sorrows, deaths and resurrections of the mystery of Marriage. The included texts are wonderful additions to worship aids, bulletins, or other resources a parish might develop for formation on the Sacrament of Matrimony.

- *Prayerbook for Engaged Couples*. 4th ed. Chicago, IL: Liturgy Training Publications, 2016. This lovely prayerbook invites and assists couples to read, discuss, and choose the Scriptures that will be proclaimed at their wedding. It also helps couples learn to pray and reflect together on

God's Word, a practice that will sustain them throughout their married lives. The book presents readings from the most recent revision of the Lectionary, prayers from the rite, and a brief reflection (with questions for discussion) on each reading and prayer.

- Turner, Paul. *Preparing the Wedding Homily: A Guide for Preachers and Couples.* Chicago, IL: Resource Publications (distributed by Liturgy Training Publications), 2003. Paul Turner, a priest and homilist, believes it is essential to involve the couple in homily preparation. His approach departs from the usual custom of picking readings first. Instead, he provides tools that help the couple think through the message they want to share and then select the most appropriate readings. Clergy and Marriage preparation teams will want to use this important tool in their ministries.

- *United in Christ: Preparing the Liturgy of the Word at Catholic Weddings.* Chicago, IL: Liturgy Training Publications, 2016. Designed as a formational tool for engaged couples, this resource provides the full text of each of the readings from *The Order of Celebrating Matrimony* with pastoral commentary. Couples can use this resource together to select the readings for their wedding liturgy. Additional ideas are provided for writing the Prayer of the Faithful and choosing particular prayers. Unlike other resources on the market, *United in Christ* presents a focused and simple resource to help couples select the most necessary parts of the wedding liturgy. The commentaries explain the meaning of the Scripture text through the lens of the needs of the couple. It is written and compiled by several authors, many of whom are married: Leisa Anslinger, Jennifer Kerr Breedlove, Charles A. Bobertz, Mary A. Ehle, Christopher J. Ferraro, Mary G. Fox, Corinna Laughlin, Biagio Mazza.

- Wuerl, Cardinal Donald. *The Marriage God Wants for You: Why the Sacrament Makes All the Difference.* Frederick, MD: The Word Among Us Press, 2015. A reflection on the meaning and the vocation of Marriage by a well-known and respected cardinal of the United States. Appropriate reading for couples and for those working with couples in the Catholic Church.

GLOSSARY

Adaptations: Changes permitted to various parts of a liturgical rite. Some adaptations are made at the national level by a conference of bishops; others can be made by the local bishop, by the pastor, or by the priest (or deacon) officiating. See also Cultural Adaptations.

Arras: A wedding custom that in some parts of the world is an exchange of coins symbolizing the couple's sharing of themselves and all their resources with each other.

Blessing: A prayer for a particular person, group of people, or thing. *The Order of Celebrating Matrimony* includes several blessing prayers, the most important of which is the Nuptial Blessing.

Bridal Party: A secular term usually referring to the flower girls, ring bearers, bridesmaids, and groomsmen, including the best man and maid or matron of honor. *The Order of Celebrating Matrimony* does not reference a bridal party or particular members of the bridal party. Instead, the rite refers to and requires two witnesses (see below). See also Wedding Party.

Catechumen: A person in the process of seeking Baptism.

Canonical Form (Form): The Marriage of two Catholics requires canonical form: the use of the ritual included in the officially approved ritual (*The Order of Celebrating Matrimony*) in the presence of a priest or deacon, the couple, and two witnesses. When a Catholic marries outside the Catholic Church, he or she needs first to obtain a dispensation (see below) from canonical form.

Consent (Vows): When exchanging the consent, a couple gives themselves to each other in Marriage, stating before the assembly their promise to be faithful and true to each other. The consent may take several forms, with the couple reciting a prescribed formula or vow, or responding to a question read by the priest or deacon with the words "I do." The consent is considered the "indispensable element that 'makes the marriage.'"[1]

---

1 CCC, 1626; CIC, 1057.

Convalidation: If a couple has a civil marriage and wishes for it to be considered sacramental, they must express their consent (share their vows) and promise their fidelity to one another in a Catholic ceremony (liturgy). This ceremony (liturgy) is called "convalidation" and it involves the giving of consent and exchange of promises in order for the marriage to be considered a sacrament. It can be done in the presence of family and friends either at Mass or outside of Mass.

Cultural Adaptations: *The Order of Celebrating Matrimony* permits a variety of cultural adaptations, changes, or additions to the rite which acknowledge the importance of certain symbolic actions in the way Marriage is celebrated in different parts of the world (see also *Arras, Lazo*).

Disparity of Cult: Refers to a marriage between a Catholic and an unbaptized person.

Dispensation: A formal release from a law or vow. In various circumstances, a couple may need to seek a dispensation from the Church in order to marry.

Evangelization (New Evangelization): The call of Christians to spread the Gospel. In the words of Bl. Pope Paul VI, the Church "exists in order to evangelize."[2] The New Evangelization, promoted by St. Pope John Paul II and subsequent pontiffs, seeks to spread the Gospel in new ways suited to the world of today.

Lazo: A wedding custom in some parts of the world, including Mexico and the Philippines, it is the placing of a cord or *lazo* (often in the form of a Rosary) over the bride and groom during the wedding liturgy. It symbolizes their life-long bond.

Marriage Preparation ("Pre-Cana"): A time of preparation for the married life for couples. It can take many forms, including weekend retreats or sessions with the pastor, another pastoral leader, or a married couple who serves as mentors or sponsors.

---

2 *Evangelii nuntiandii*, 14.

Matrimony: The sacrament by which a man and woman enter into the state of Marriage. The Church uses both terms in the rite, but prefers the term "Matrimony" to refer to the sacrament itself. The full title of the rite is *The Order of Celebrating Matrimony.*

Mixed Religion Marriage (see also Disparity of Cult): Refers to a Marriage between a Catholic and a baptized non-Catholic.

Nave: The main body of a church building. The word comes from the Latin *navis*, or ship, which the body of a church was thought to resemble.

Nuptial Blessing: The solemn blessing of the couple and an important part of *The Order of Celebrating Matrimony.* When the Marriage takes place within the Mass, the Nuptial Blessing is prayed over the couple after the Lord's Prayer and before the Sign of Peace is exchanged. When the *Order of Celebrating Matrimony* is celebrated outside of Mass, the Nuptial Blessing concludes the Prayer of the Faithful.

Nuptial Mass: A wedding that takes place during Mass.

Order: See Rite.

The Order of Celebrating Matrimony: The ritual by which men and women are joined in Marriage. It includes readings, prayers, and rubrics (instructions) for the celebration of the Sacrament of Matrimony. Formerly called the *Rite of Marriage.*

Praenotanda: Latin for "pre-notes," this term refers to the prefatory material found in the various ritual books of the Church. These instructions often include theological reflection on the rite as well as additional detail on how the rites are to be carried out.

Procession: Any time a group of people move from one place to another in the liturgy, it is called a procession. The primary processions during the liturgy are the Entrance Procession, as the priest and other ministers enter the church at the beginning of the liturgy; the Gospel Procession, when the priest or deacon moves to the ambo to proclaim the Gospel; the procession of gifts, when the bread and wine are brought forward for the celebration of the Eucharist; the Communion Procession, as the assembly moves forward to receive Holy Communion; and the concluding procession (sometimes called the "recessional") at the end of Mass. During a wedding liturgy, the bride and groom take part in the liturgical procession accompanied by their witnesses and usually their parents.

Rite: Refers to the order by which a ritual is carried out. The Catholic Church has rites which govern the celebration of the Mass and other sacraments and sacramentals.

Ritual: A sequence of actions carried out for a significant purpose. There are many religious, civic, and military rituals. In Catholic life, ritual is key to how we worship and experience the sacraments.

Ritual Books: The books including the prayers, readings, and instructions for celebrating the rituals of the Church. These include the *Lectionary for Mass*, *The Roman Missal*, and *The Order of Celebrating Matrimony*, along with many others.

Ritual Gesture: A wordless gesture which is a meaningful part of a liturgical rite. For example, the priest or deacon extending both hands over the couple during the Nuptial Blessing is an important ritual gesture in the *Order of Celebrating Matrimony*.

Solemnity: The most important days in the Church's liturgical calendar are called solemnities. These include Sundays, Holydays of Obligation such as the Assumption of the Blessed Virgin Mary (August 15) and the Immaculate Conception (December 8), and other observances such as for Sts. Peter and Paul (June 29), among others. When weddings are celebrated on solemnities, the readings and prayers of the day must be used. Because of the importance of the Scriptures in the understanding of the Sacrament of Matrimony, however, one of the readings from *The Order of Celebrating Matrimony* may be chosen on many solemnities, except from Holy Thursday to Easter, Epiphany, Ascension, Pentecost, Corpus Christi, and holydays of obligation. However, on Feasts of the Lord or of the saints — observances which rank lower than solemnities — the entire wedding Mass may be used, with all the texts drawn from the choices from *The Order of Celebrating Matrimony*.

Statement of Intentions: Before the consent, the priest or deacon asks the couple several questions about their freedom of choice, their willingness to be faithful to each other, and their openness to children (this last question is omitted for older couples). If either party cannot answer yes to any one of these questions, they will not be able to enter into a valid Catholic Marriage.

Sunday: The "Lord's Day," dedicated to rest and worship. The Sunday liturgy is the high point of the week. When weddings are celebrated on Sundays at a parish Mass, the proper prayers of the day must be used, and couples may select one reading from *The Order of Celebrating Matrimony* in place of the prescribed readings of the day. However, in Ordinary Time and Christmas Time, the entire wedding liturgy, with reading and prayers, can be used at a Sunday wedding as long as it is not a regular parish Mass.

Sign/Symbol: "In human life, signs and symbols occupy an important place. As a being at once body and spirit, man expresses and pe=rceives spiritual realities through physical signs and symbols."[3] The liturgy is full of symbolic elements; in fact, all the Church's sacramental celebrations are "woven from signs and symbols."[4] We usually use the word "sign" to refer to objects which point to higher realities—in the wedding ritual, the rings are a sign of the couple's lifetime commitment to one another. The word *symbol* refers to larger realities of faith. Marriage itself is spoken of as a symbol of Christ's union with the Church he loves.

Veil: A piece of fine cloth or lace worn over the head. In Western cultures the bridal veil has had a variety of symbolic meanings, none of them integral to the wedding liturgy. It has been taken to allude to virginity, or as a reference to the customary head covering worn by women in churches in past ages. It continues to be a traditional part of wedding attire, though the meaning continues to evolve. The veil is not always associated only with the bride. In some cultural traditions a veil is unfolded over both bride and groom during the wedding rite, representing the single roof they will share as a married couple.

Vocation: From the Latin *vocare*, "to call," vocation refers to the sense of God's call to a particular way of life. The Church views married life as well as priesthood or religious life as special vocations, to which God calls some of his people. The *Catechism of the Catholic Church* defines Marriage and Holy Orders as the sacraments of vocation.[5]

Wedding Party: See Witnesses and Bridal Party.

Witnesses: The Church requires two witnesses to be present at the Marriage liturgy. Usually, the best man and the maid or matron of honor serve as the official witnesses. See also Bridal Party.

---

3 CCC, 1146.
4 CCC, 1145.
5 See CCC, 1534–35.

ACKNOWLEDGMENTS

Scripture texts are from the *New American Bible*, revised edition © 2010, 1991, 1986, 1970 Confraternity of Christian Doctrine, Washington, DC. Used with permission. All rights reserved. No part of the *New American Bible* may be reproduced without permission in writing from the copyright owner

Excerpts from *Built of Living Stones: Art, Architecture, and Worship* © 2000, United States Catholic Conference, Inc., Washington, DC. All rights reserved. Excerpts from *Sing to the Lord: Music in Divine Worship* © 2008 United States Conference of Catholic Bishops, Washington, DC. Used with permission. All rights reserved. Excerpts from *Preaching the Mystery of Faith* © 2012, United States Conference of Catholic Bishops, Washington, DC. Used with permission. All rights reserved.

Excerpts from the English translation of the *Catechism of the Catholic Church for the United States of America* © 1994, United States Catholic Conference, Inc. — Libreria Editrice Vaticana. English translation of the *Catechism of the Catholic Church Modifications from the Editio Typica* © 1997, United States Catholic Conference, Inc. — Libreria Editrice Vaticana. Used with permission.

Excerpts from the English translation of *Amoris laetitia*, *Evangelii gaudium*, and the address from Pope Francis to the bishops of the United States are reprinted with the kind permission of Libreria Editrice Vaticana.

Excerpts from the English translation of *Rite of Marriage* © 1969 (superseded), International Commission on English in the Liturgy Corporation (ICEL); excerpts from *Documents on the Liturgy, 1963-1979: Conciliar, Papal, and Curial Texts* © 1982, ICEL; excerpts from the English translation of *Rite of Christian Initiation of Adults* © 1985, ICEL; excerpts from the English translation of *The Roman Missal* © 2010, ICEL; excerpts from the English translation of *The Order of Celebrating Matrimony* © 2013, ICEL. All rights reserved. Texts contained in this work derived whole or in part from liturgical texts copyrighted by the International Commission on English in the Liturgy (ICEL) have been published here with the confirmation of the Committee on Divine Worship, United States Conference of Catholic Bishops. No other texts in this work have been formally reviewed or approved by the United States Conference of Catholic Bishops.

Excerps from *Ritual del Matrimonio* © 2006 Comisión Episcopal de Pastoral Litúrgica de la Conferencia del Episcopado Mexicano; *Leccionario III* © 1993 Comisión Episcopal de Pastoral Litúrgica de la Conferencia del Episcopado Mexicano. All rights reserved.

Excerpts from *Documents of the Marriage Liturgy*, by Mark Searle and Kenneth W. Stevenson reprinted with the kind permission of the family estate.